Succeed with the Standards in Your Social Studies Classroom

Margaret A. Laughlin   and   **H. Michael Hartoonian**

University of Wisconsin
Green Bay

University of Minnesota
Minneapolis

J. WESTON

WALCH
PUBLISHER

Portland, Maine

User's Guide
to
Walch Reproducible Books

As part of our general effort to provide educational materials that are as practical and economical as possible, we have designated this publication a "reproducible book." The designation means that purchase of the book includes purchase of the right to limited reproduction of all pages on which this symbol appears:

Here is the basic Walch policy: We grant to individual purchasers of this book the right to make sufficient copies of reproducible pages for use by all students of a single teacher. This permission is limited to a single teacher, and does not apply to entire schools or school systems, so institutions purchasing the book should pass the permission on to a single teacher. Copying of the book or its parts for resale is prohibited.

Any questions regarding this policy or requests to purchase further reproduction rights should be addressed to:

Permissions Editor
J. Weston Walch, Publisher
321 Valley Street • P. O. Box 658
Portland, Maine 04104-0658

1   2   3   4   5   6   7   8   9   10
ISBN 0-8251-3333-5

Contents

Acknowledgments and Dedication

The authors wish to acknowledge the significant contributions that the members of the National Council for the Social Studies Task Force on Standards have made to the field of social studies education. The members developed the 10 NCSS standards (themes), described performance expectations, and provided teachers with examples that focus on ways teachers are able to transform the standards into classroom practices. During the development of *Expectations for Excellence,* more than 2,000 teachers participated in the field-testing of the themes, performance expectations, and classroom examples. At this time, thousands of PK–12 teachers and students are using these standards to enhance quality social studies teaching and learning throughout the United States and elsewhere.

In addition, the authors extend their appreciation to Lisa French, Pam O'Neil, and Jeanelle Beaulieu at J. Weston Walch, Publisher, for their valuable assistance in the development of the book and its publication. Thanks to everyone involved.

This book is dedicated to the community of scholars who make up our profession.

Preface

During the recent past, various professional organizations have developed national standards in several disciplines, or are in the process of developing standards. The National Council for the Social Studies (NCSS) is no exception and has developed ten standards (themes) for social studies teachers to use to develop curriculum, link curriculum and assessment, select instructional resources, and provide opportunities for staff development. The ten NCSS standards developed by the Social Studies Task Force on Standards are the following:

I.	Culture
II.	Time, Continuity, and Change
III.	People, Places, and Environments
IV.	Individual Development and Identity
V.	Individuals, Groups, and Institutions
VI.	Power, Authority, and Governance
VII.	Production, Distribution, and Consumption
VIII.	Science, Technology, and Society
IX.	Global Connections
X.	Civic Ideals and Practices

The themes represent the seven social science disciplines most often associated with social studies—anthropology, history, geography, psychology, sociology, political science, and economics—and three interdisciplinary themes: science, technology, and society; global connections; and civic ideals and practices. These themes reflect social studies content and concepts that are generally agreed upon as being important by social science discipline specialists and members of the social studies profession. Ideally, the themes will be addressed throughout the PK–12 school years, with some standards receiving a greater emphasis than others during a particular course or unit of instruction.

Social studies is both a single discipline and a multi-oriented discipline. For example, the history standard asks students to study the relationships between past and present, people and events, and their significance to the local, state, national, and international communities. The people, places, and environments standard asks students to view the world from the perspective of geography. The three behavioral sciences standards—anthropology, psychology, and sociology—deal with the design and purpose of human institutions such as family and church and help us to integrate our personal lives to the larger community, which is becoming ever more diverse. Both political science and economics are policy-oriented disciplines that help students make important personal and social policy decisions. The interdisciplinary content themes embedded in the standards allow students to compare various methodologies from the perspective of several social science disciplines and to draw on content from the arts and humanities, philosophy, mathematics, the natural sciences, and law when studying a particular current issue or long-standing problem.

The book is organized into five chapters. It includes background information about the standards and suggests ways middle and high school teachers can use the standards as they help young people learn about important social studies concepts and skills. Chapter 1 provides a rationale for standards. Chapter 2 discusses issues related to social studies programs. Chapter 3 indicates the important role of assessment in monitoring student learning and providing quality social studies programs. Chapter 4 includes examples of student learning activities with sample reproducible pages, which are useful in helping students become active learners and effective citizens in our democracy. Chapter 5 identifies several social studies-related professional organizations with which social studies teachers should become familiar.

Introduction

Curriculum and Content Standards:
Perspectives on Knowing, Learning, and Teaching

We are living in a time when most of us are moving from one economic epoch toward another. No longer an industrial society, and not yet sure of the emerging global economic landscape, we seem to be living in a time between the times: Our disorientation forces us to ask fundamental questions about our lives, our identity, what we should teach, and what it is that students should learn.

Over the course of history, this kind of unease has occurred, in one form or another, every time that we have created and confronted a major shift in ideological thought and economic practice. And these revolutions have always been preceded and accompanied by a set of attending issues, revolving around the nature of knowledge and how we come to know. The social and personal manifestations of this environmental stress are everywhere apparent today, raising such questions as: What knowledge is of most worth? Whose knowledge is of most worth? How can I bring meaning to my life in a time when information and knowledge are rapidly increasing and changing fundamental precepts about how the world works? How do cultural perspectives influence the nature of what we know? Is knowledge discovered or created? Given the nature of knowledge, what kind of work will I do in the future? Where will I live? How will I live?

These are the types of knowledge questions that seem to surface in human discourse during times of great social disruptions and economic dislocations. This would certainly be the case today, as we seem to be defining the new social order and economy in terms of global information and global connections.

In response to perceptions of our changing need to know, and the attending knowledge questions, our educational, economic, and social institutions prepare standards to assure us that they are dealing with the right or best content. A standard is a benchmark against which we can compare ideas and things for the purpose of determining accuracy, judging quality, or measuring quantity. Standards suggest modes of behavior and intellectual virtues that point us toward a higher content—or, at least, a content more useful to the coming age. Within a democratic society, however, we all need to address these questions, for their public policy extensions will determine the nature of our schools, the outlook of our communities, and the quality of our lives.

This book addresses fundamental questions about standards in the field of social studies, and will show how standards can link teaching and learning. The ten themes of the National Council for the Social Studies that form the foundation for content standards in the several social sciences and integrated subject area fields of social studies are used in two different ways. First of all, the themes provide an organizing framework for the curriculum. Second, the themes help provide a focus for instruction and assessment. Throughout the book, attention is given to how we come to know about the world and ourselves, and how different disciplines, as well as linguistic and cultural perspectives, add to the complexities and richness of meaning. Within the several themes, we also address fundamental questions about the activities of people, giving texture to the ways in which we use knowledge in our daily lives. For example:

- How do people create beauty in their lives?
- How do people deal with time?
- How do people organize themselves in order to provide for basic economic wants and needs?

Finally, the application of these curriculum and instructional ideas will help us address some larger issues about our society and schools in a time of change. The concept of content standards provides a dynamic context for addressing the following questions:

- Can—and should—a common curriculum be constructed?
- Can the "common school" be a reality in the future of the United States of America?
- Can there be a united nation without a common understanding of knowledge?
- Can knowledge give us the ability to know who we are in relationship to one another and to society?
- Can attention to standards help our instructional program (particularly with regard to student achievement and meaning)?

The primary purpose of this book is to create a context in which to explore these questions, to enhance the life of the mind, and to think more clearly about the power of knowledge relative to our learning communities. Thus, as we create content standards and think about their use in designing, learning, and assessment programs, we will also develop new conceptions of knowledge, a process fundamental to professional growth.

—M.A.L.
—H.M.H.

Chapter 1

The Use of Standards in Teaching and Learning Social Studies

Teachers open the door . . . you enter by yourself.

—Confucius (c. 500 B.C.)

Why Are Standards Needed?

Needs vary, depending on the context in which we find ourselves. When we think about curriculum and content standards and why they are necessary, we must understand standards within a social, political, economic, and cultural context. Our society's underlying need for standards comes from a deep feeling that things are out of control and that we must do a better job of structuring our lives and minds. Some would add that the feeling of need reflects a distrust of teachers, of texts, and of the ability of local education officials to understand content and curriculum issues. Over the last twenty years or so, education has become more and more of a political issue. The political element is fed by news stories on low student test scores, increasing school violence, the escalating cost of education, and the failure of the United States to hold its own in the global marketplace.

We believe that the effective use of standards in social studies programs can enrich our craft in four important ways.

First, standards can provide an excellent set of criteria for professional growth. Standards give us the defining elements that help us keep our knowledge base current, complete, and correct. We have an opportunity to study, reflect, and act upon those elements as we seek a better understanding of our discipline.

Second, standards present a framework of knowledge that helps us construct a curriculum based on the most powerful content ideas (what we call the *integrity of the curriculum scope*).

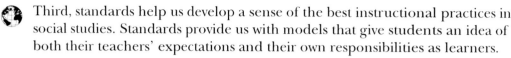 Third, standards help us develop a sense of the best instructional practices in social studies. Standards provide us with models that give students an idea of both their teachers' expectations and their own responsibilities as learners.

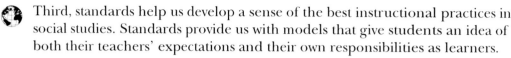 Finally, standards help us evaluate both our students' and our own efforts and achievements as measured against the best criteria and practices of our profession.

In summary, standards present us with an opportunity to work toward an agreement among students and educators that will define our reciprocal duties as scholars and as citizens and enable us to construct a more meaningful, ongoing learning community rooted in a common purpose.

Using Curriculum and Content Standards to Design Professional Growth Activities

We should not overlook the application of national standards to the process of professional growth when designing strategies for improving curriculum and instruction. We can teach only what we know. Standards can help us evaluate our content base, as well as our conception of knowledge. They can also help us check our current understanding of the developmental readiness of students and the design of our instructional programs. We assert that the half-life of a baccalaureate degree is about two years or less, and that information is doubling every four to seven years. Against this reality, it becomes necessary to evalu-

> *We assert that the half-life of a baccalaureate degree is about two years or less, and that information is doubling every four to seven years.*

ate continually our professional growth experiences to determine what information and practices to keep, what to discard, and what to revise or reconstruct. While standards cannot do this task for us, they will certainly help create a framework where this important work can be accomplished.

Given the structure of most schools, we teachers seldom have an opportunity to reflect upon the principles of content and teaching that form the foundation of the PK–12 social studies program. Curriculum frameworks are based on the assumption that specific decisions about scope and sequence are out of our hands. The system generally does not operate as a democratic community of scholars, and such decisions are fundamentally political. Thus, we often remove ourselves from the discussion and the decision-making process. We see our knowledge, concerns, and efforts as having little hope of survival in the nondemocratic marketplace of ideas. Curriculum decisions are generally made by an individual, or a small group of people within the state or local authority power structure. This process often lacks a common set of principles or standards from either the national professional associations or local teachers. Ultimately, we are left to interpret and implement someone else's ideas, which we neither own nor reinforce. The result is a curriculum design for the PK–12 social studies program that is neither unified nor comprehensive. We are left with fourteen separate programs that end up being fragmented, redundant, and boring to both teachers and students.

How can we construct a workable approach to curriculum design and professional growth? The approach must be based upon necessary and manageable themes and questions that can initiate a dialogue. The dialogue must address the logical, philosophical, and historical relevance of teaching ideals.

One purpose of the national standards for social studies is to serve as a guide for curriculum decisions. This purpose is accomplished by providing performance expectations regarding knowledge, processes, and attitudes essential for all students. The standards focus our discussion on content and teaching practices, ultimately providing a common set of ideas about the task of curriculum building. The standards provide us with criteria for considering issues such as why teach social studies, what is to be included in the curriculum, how to teach social studies well to all students, and how to assess whether students are able to apply what they have learned about social studies in the real world. The standards communicate to students, parents, colleagues, and the commuity the nature of a quality program.

> *The first step in program improvement is not with the program itself, but with the individuals who will design and implement the program.*

Before starting any curriculum improvement efforts, we should read and discuss the national standards in several social science disciplines—not for reasons of application in the curriculum, but for reasons of personal and professional growth. The first step in program improvement is not with the program itself, but with the individuals who will design and implement the program.

Using Curriculum and Content Standards as a Framework of Knowledge

We understand knowledge to be a human construct. That is, what we know is based upon a dynamic structure designed by people as they try to understand how the world works. This changing map of the intellectual landscape is always in the process of being reconceptualized and validated. These frameworks of knowledge shape our understanding of each other and the world.

Standards present us with a knowledge framework. At the same time, they encourage us to construct new frameworks. For example, the national social studies standards can be used to organize content within a curriculum field. A community of several hundred people, all with a high degree of expertise in the discipline of social studies, constructed a framework to describe the field. They presented a state-of-the-art design of content. But, in and of themselves, the standards are not dynamic. Without educators and students who are knowledgeable and willing to engage and use them in their craft, standards are without utility, except as a defining political statement. It is the use, application, and connection of standards to the practice of scholarship that makes them valuable. Through this use, individuals and groups are constantly constructing new frameworks. To be sure, these new and developing frameworks are only new at the margins of the disciplines; however, they represent the expanding edge of curriculum and instructional development. In a real sense, the standards can serve as a dynamic link between current practice and the desire for improvement that drives all scholarship.

Guiding Questions

- What conceptions of knowledge do we hold, and what relationship do these views have with our curriculum design and instructional patterns?

- What procedures do we use to update the knowledge base of the curriculum?

- How can the standards enrich the content of our curriculum?

- How can the standards help us decide what to include and to exclude from the scope of our program?

Using Curriculum and Content Standards to Improve Instructional Practice

We believe that *how* we teach is directly related to *what* we teach. Content drives the instructional design in the way that the landscape (environment) dictates the shelter and clothing of a region. The nature of disciplines such as economics and political science suggests that any instructional program will include opportunities for policy design, evaluation, and implementation. Geography will almost always include attention to models, maps, and the interrelationships between natural and human systems. History lends itself to multiple interpretations of topics or themes over time, and to a study of the ways evidence is located and used. The behavioral sciences provide opportunities for us to study human behaviors in various settings and cultures. The point is that each discipline within social studies, as well as its integration, suggests methods and instructional practices that flow naturally from the content. We should make the most of this reality. As we study and implement the standards that are presented in the following chapters, we will have many opportunities to see and use the dynamic relationship between content and instructional practices.

The point is that each discipline within social studies . . . suggests methods and instructional practices that flow naturally from the content.

Guiding Questions

- What relationships can we construct between *how* and *what* is taught?
- How would you describe your conception of knowledge? of information?
- How is information presented to students? Is knowledge presented or constructed in different ways?
- How can we know whether students understand content? whether our objectives have been met?

Using Curriculum and Content Standards to Evaluate Student Achievement

We believe that comprehension is based on at least two necessary elements: knowledge of a rich content vocabulary and the logical arguments from premises to conclusions. This suggests that any evaluation of student progress should measure both the conceptual understanding that students have and how they think about the relationships between premises and conclusions.

Students acquire a working set of concepts, as well as a structure from which to begin building connections among these concepts. Student achievement is assessed in three different, yet related, ways: first, whether students understand the concepts or working vocabulary of the subject; second, whether students can construct and apply knowledge of the subject to questions, issues, and concerns relating to topics of personal or social importance; third, whether students understand, create, and apply connections among subject fields and between scholarly content and everyday practices.

Guiding Questions

- How would you define or describe the differences between instructional practices and evaluation design?
- How can standards provide a benchmark for evaluation?
- Who should be involved in making judgments about student achievement, program quality, and teacher effectiveness?

Your reflections on the social studies standards and the guiding questions are the tools to help construct, implement, and evaluate quality social studies programs.

Chapter 2

Social Studies: Creating a Context for Excellence

I know of no safe depository of the ultimate powers of the society but with the people themselves; and if we think them not enlightened enough to exercise their control with a wholesome discretion, the remedy is not to take power from them, but to inform their discretion through instruction.

—Thomas Jefferson (1820)

A Rationale

Education must always be defined within the value structure of a particular society, primarily because education is responsible for maintaining the cultural heritage and improving self and society. This means attending to the interrelated goals of education for self-development, citizenship, and employment. In a democratic republic, education is even more critical since our system is built upon the concept of the "enlightened citizen."

> **In a democratic republic, education is even more critical since our system is built upon the concept of the "enlightened citizen."**

Such individuals are in touch with our cultural heritage. They possess a working knowledge of the economic, political, and social factors that make up the human ecosystem in which we all must function. They understand the principles of rule of law, legal limits to freedom, cooperation, and the demand for quality in the character and work of themselves and others. Without a conscious effort to teach and learn these things, a free republic will not long endure. Thus, our first priority, our first public policy goal, is to ensure our survival as a free nation through the development of enlightened citizens.

Within this context, the school plays a dominant role; within the general school curriculum, social studies is the most fundamental program at all grade levels. This responsibility is placed here because no one else on the teaching staff is better qualified, and no other curriculum area is better organized, to assume this task.

Social studies is concerned with developing reflective, democratic citizenship within a national and global context. Social studies includes the disciplines typically classified as belonging to the social and behavioral sciences, as well as history, geography, and content selected from law, philosophy, and the humanities. It also includes those topics that focus on social problems, issues, and controversies. Social studies is both single-discipline and multidiscipline oriented, depending upon the objectives being pursued. Social studies addresses five educational goals:

1. Enlightened democratic citizenship in order to participate effectively in local, state, national, and international affairs

2. Appreciation and understanding of our cultural heritage and its role in contemporary society

3. Acquisition of knowledge and skills related to the study of people's individual and group behaviors in a variety of places and times, with particular attention to motivations and consequences

4. The joy of learning about self, others, and human history

5. Learning how to learn—how to understand complex ideas and how to create new ideas

All of these goals are equal in importance, for they reinforce each other. Thus, the goal of citizenship is supported by the goals of disciplined academic study and knowing how to continue to learn. In other words, the student should be able to:

1. Use reasoning processes in economic, political, and social decision making

2. Comprehend the vocabulary, logic, and methodology of the several academic subject areas that make up social studies

3. Communicate ideas through speaking, listening, writing, and the use of other symbols

4. Use the methods (languages) of the social sciences, history, literature, social mathematics (statistics and computer science), and the fine arts to describe and explain social phenomena

Most importantly, a thorough understanding of social studies can provide for the development of *perspective*. Perspective is an understanding or

> *. . . a thorough understanding of social studies can provide for the development of* **perspective.**

wisdom gained by a knowledge of history that transcends the present setting and allows one the courage to ask questions such as, What is the good society? What is the good person? What obligations do I have to the ideals and people of the past, present, and future? What is the proper relationship between the individual and the state? How and to what extent should I be involved with the rest of the people on this globe? Can our civilization endure? What values do we wish to preserve?

The social studies teacher must be a student of the social studies discipline, contemporary affairs, and the history and philosophy of education. Knowledge and skill in using various instructional approaches, materials, and media are essential. Awareness and sensitivity to the complex nature of human interactions are also required.

Social studies teachers need a liberal (general) education as a base for intellectual independence and rational behavior. This should include work in the humanities and arts, social sciences, natural sciences, mathematics, and foreign languages. Social studies teachers should study in considerable depth at least one culture different from their own. They should have a world or global view concerning people's problems. They should also be articulate relative to the human condition.

Along with their liberal (general) studies, social studies teachers should have extensive knowledge in areas of academic specialization and professional education. Social studies teachers must also continue to learn about and understand the complexities of being a social studies teacher in a modern democratic republic. This means, above all, keeping up-to-date with the social studies profession and contributing to it so as to continually improve school programs.

> *. . . we can teach only what we know and who we are.*

In many ways the attention to professional growth is a fundamental rationale for the study and implementation of curriculum and content standards. This is written in the belief that we can teach only what we know and who we are. Standards can provide an opportunity to enhance this knowledge.

Program Scope: Major Curriculum Themes

The scope of the quality social studies program is constructed on the ten themes of social studies as identified by the National Council for the Social Studies and listed in Figure 1.

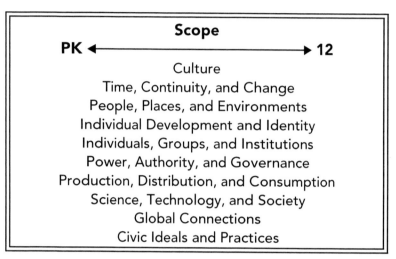

Scope

PK ←————————————→ **12**

Culture
Time, Continuity, and Change
People, Places, and Environments
Individual Development and Identity
Individuals, Groups, and Institutions
Power, Authority, and Governance
Production, Distribution, and Consumption
Science, Technology, and Society
Global Connections
Civic Ideals and Practices

Figure 1

The National Council for the Social Studies has defined the themes and their focus as follows: Culture (anthropology); Time, Continuity, and Change (history); People, Places, and Environments (geography); Individual Development and Identity (psychology); Individuals, Groups, and Institutions (sociology); Power, Authority, and Governance (political science); Production, Distribution, and Consumption (economics); Science, Technology, and Society (multidisciplinary); Global Connections (multidisciplinary); and Civic Ideals and Practices (multidisciplinary).

The social studies standards will help teachers, program and curriculum designers, and administrators at the state, district, and school-site levels develop a systematic PK–12 social studies program. Using the social studies standards as an "umbrella" can assist program development by:

🌐 Ensuring integrated, cumulative social studies learning at each level (that is, learning that addresses powerful discipline-based and interdisciplinary themes at the early, intermediate, middle, and high school levels)

🌐 Encouraging program designers to use inclusive social studies themes as the basis for a curriculum design that can also draw upon other standards projects (for example, history, geography, civics, and economics) for specific grade levels or courses within the PK–12 programs as appropriate. Most importantly, the several social science disciplines thus find a curriculum "home" in social studies, since no one discipline is sufficient in and of itself to meet the vision of social studies as an integrative field.

A metaphor can help readers conceptualize the relationship between social studies and specific, individual disciplines as they promote learning in a PK–12 social studies program. Consider a musical ensemble such as an orchestra (the social studies program) as it performs a specific musical composition (a grade level or specific course within the curriculum). At certain times, one instrument (a discipline such as history) takes the lead while others (such as geography and economics) play supporting roles. At other times, several instruments (history, geography, etc.) or the full ensemble play together to fully address the composer's thematic aims. The quality of the performance is the result of the composer's creation of the music (design of the social studies curriculum), the unique qualities of individual instruments (the contributions of individual disciplines), the acoustics of the setting (expertise of curriculum planners and teachers, school site facilities, and instructional resources), and the skills of musicians and the conductor (students, teachers, program planners, and implementers) to know when and how to express the meaning of the composition (curriculum).

There is a rational relationship between the social studies standards and the standards of the several social sciences. The social studies standards address the overall curriculum design and the comprehensive student performance expectations of a program of excellence, while the individual sets of discipline standards provide enhanced content detail to ensure quality instructional programs. Teachers and curriculum designers are encouraged, first, to establish their program frameworks, using the social studies standards as a guide, and then to use the individual sets of standards from history, geography, civics, economics, or other disciplines (science, mathematics, foreign language, and the arts) to guide the development of strands and courses within their programs. Using these standards in concert with one another can enable educators to give adequate attention to both integrated and single-discipline configurations within the social studies curriculum.

The effective use of the social studies curriculum standards will depend not only on the quality of their design, but also on the skills of educators to know when and how to integrate content, to design quality learning environments, and to construct with these standards more complete PK–12 social studies programs that reflect the newest research in learning, developmental abilities of students, and knowledge construction. Only such a thoughtfully designed curriculum will carry forth a vision of social studies for the next century.

Program Sequence: Major Content Focus

Many social studies scope-and-sequence models recommend a spiral or expanding-horizon content approach, starting with the immediate, familiar, and concrete environment in the primary grades and moving outward to the more distant and abstract in high school. The design outlined in Figure 2 is a somewhat similar organizational pattern except that its content focus is organized on the basis of grade-level clusters developed around the ten major curriculum themes described in Fgure 1. Teachers are encouraged to talk with one another across and within grade-level clusters about social studies content, concepts, abilities, and values.

In organizing the curriculum within each grade-level cluster, students and teachers are asked to address a series of broad-content focus questions that allow gathering, integrating, and interpreting data from multiple sources, developing higher-order thinking, and making reasoned judgments about each finding.

The suggested questions can be used to construct content and to identify key concepts and topics for the PK–12 instructional program. Further, these questions can be used to encourage students and teachers to become active inquirers seeking to find answers or solutions, however tentative, to these questions, issues, concerns, and topics. Teachers and students are urged to grapple intellectually with these questions to facilitate learning for both the teachers and students. Both students and teachers need to model thinking and explain why they responded as they did. Teachers need to talk about how they came to the conclusions they did and, if they change their conclusions, to explain how and why they changed their ideas and opinions based on the acquisition of new knowledge and/or further reflection. At the same time, students and teachers need to be open to new ideas and information as they become available.

The grade-level clusters are organized with the content focus shown in Figure 2.

Suggested Grade-Level Clusters	
Grade Level	*Content Focus*
Primary Grades (PK–2)	My Orientation to the World
Intermediate Grades (3–5)	Expanding My World Horizons
Middle School Grades (6–8)	Viewing the World from Different Perspectives
Secondary Grades (9–12)	Assuming Full Citizenship in a Changing World

Figure 2

Within each of the grade-level clusters, illustrative examples of broad focus questions representing the ten themes are used to organize the curriculum. Naturally, many other questions could be posed—and numerous related questions could be formulated—within each of the broad question categories. The choice of questions to be used in determining content is the responsibility of the local curriculum committee.

In the following section, the authors briefly identify key characteristics of learners at various grade-level clusters and offer several illustrative examples of student activities to encourage active learning and skill development We do not, then, answer questions such as, should a unit on Mexico or Latin America be taught in the fifth or sixth grade? We believe that, in truth, it does not make much difference. The important thing to keep in mind is that we must teach about *substantive content* and that it must be *current, accurate, and comprehensive*. Grade-level assignments of topics are important, as they provide for the elimination of gaps and overlaps in the scope and sequence. But a curriculum plan is a good deal more. A curriculum plan is fundamentally a way for teachers to communicate with one another and the larger community as well.

The Learner and Curriculum Content

While the focus of this book is on middle and high school social studies, it is important that teachers in these grades have a knowledge of the content and questions asked of students in primary and intermediate grades. Illustrative examples at the earlier grade-level clusters are included in this chapter.

Primary Students (Grades PK–2)

Students in the primary grades bring to social studies classes a variety of previous experiences that form the foundations for learning and help determine their intellectual, social, emotional, and physical growth. The social studies program at these grade levels should enable students to move from a largely egocentric view of the world toward developing an understanding of their roles and responsibilities in their families, in their schools, and in various social institutions and settings.

In these grades, it is important to provide a variety of meaningful, firsthand, concrete learning experiences that draw upon experiences from the home, school, neighborhood, and the world beyond. For example, opportunities should be provided that allow students to develop social participation skills through committee work, role-playing, creative dramatics, greeting classroom visitors, classroom discussion, and informational interviews; to practice research skills by gathering and recording information from various sources such as films, pictures, stories, music, and field trips; to develop citizenship skills through sharing, by accepting responsibility for their own actions through cooperative planning, making compromises, resolving conflicts, and making decisions; and to enhance communication skills through drawing, reading, writing, listening, and speaking activities.

Within this grade-level cluster, students need to have opportunities for individual as well as group-learning activities. Appropriate to their maturity level, students should be introduced to concepts and values from the several social studies disciplines through varied concrete learning experiences that will lead to active citizenship participation. There should be numerous opportunities to celebrate and take pride in our cultural heritage by focusing on state, national, and ethnic holidays included in the social studies curriculum.

My Orientation to the World (Grades PK–2)	
Theme	**Theme Content Questions**
Culture	What can I learn about myself? What is expected of me? What can I learn about others?
Time, Continuity, and Change	What is special about my community? How has my community changed over the years?
People, Places, and Environments	How can I describe my environment at home, at school, and in my neighborhood? How do these environments influence my life?
Individual Development and Identity	Who am I? What can I learn about myself while I am learning about other people?
Individuals, Groups, and Institutions	What is a family? What traditions and events do we celebrate in my family? Why are they important?
Power, Authority, and Governance	Why do we need rules at home, at school, and in my neighborhood to limit what we do? What rights do I have?
Production, Distribution, and Consumption	How can I meet my basic wants? What goods and services are available to me?
Science, Technology, and Society	How has technology changed the way I live compared with the way my parents and grandparents lived when they were my age?
Global Connections	What can I learn about other people and cultures through creative drama, stories, art, music, and games from other countries?
Civic Ideals and Practices	How can I be a good citizen? What are good citizenship practices? What are some good citizenship habits to develop?

Intermediate Students (Grades 3–5)

The social studies curriculum for this grade-level cluster provides an opportunity for interdisciplinary study of our community, state, and nation, with attention given to our culture, environment, people, challenges, and successes. By studying the community, state, and nation, students have the opportunity to learn such concepts as diversity, environment, migration, urbanization, transportation, heritage, ethnicity, technology, and beliefs. They also learn about institutional variables such as family, government, economy, and education in selected settings at various times and in different cultures; that provides a foundation for ongoing learning.

 Students should explore a variety of print and nonprint resources to learn about their cultural, geographic, economic, political, and historical heritage. Most students also enjoy reading and studying the biographies of great and common women and men in various geographical and historical settings. Children's literature, music, and art provide opportunities to integrate social studies with other aspects of the school program. Other excellent sources for data include field trips to museums, historic sites, local businesses, agricultural centers, governmental agencies, and environmental areas. Students also enjoy hearing guest speakers tell about exciting topics in an interesting manner, perhaps with the use of artifacts or other visuals or by using music and art in their presentations.

Students in these grades need to engage in numerous activities, experiences, and opportunities to refine and develop previously learned skills. They also need to develop new learning skills, including inquiry and research skills from ever-widening sources, to develop critical-thinking and problem-solving abilities. Numerous opportunities for meaningful individualized, small-group, and entire-group instruction should be offered throughout the year so that students have the opportunity to develop knowledge and skills needed for productive living and learning.

Expanding My World Horizons (Grades 3–5)	
Theme	*Theme Content Questions*
Culture	What are some examples of the contributions of ethnic and cultural groups in our community, state, and nation? What do we have in common?
Time, Continuity, and Change	What are some important documents that have shaped our history? How have they influenced our past and our present way of life?
People, Places, and Environments	What are some special geographic features of our landscape? What physical features influence the location of communities around the world?
Individual Development and Identity	What are some of my talents? What are some of my interests? What are some possible careers that I might enjoy?
Individuals, Groups, and Institutions	How do communities show diversity? How are communities similar? How have communities changed over time?
Power, Authority, and Governance	How do laws provide for stability, justice, and control in our daily lives?
Production, Distribution, and Consumption	How do ideas, people, and products circulate in our community, state, and nation? How do people in our region interact with people in other regions?
Science, Technology, and Society	How has technology changed the way we live? How is technology likely to help shape our future?
Global Connections	How do our community, state, and nation rely on people in other parts of the world?
Civic Ideals and Practices	What are some characteristics of a good community and a good citizen? How can I be a good citizen? What do citizens have in common?

Middle School Students (Grades 6–8)

Middle school students are at an age of transition that includes rapid physical growth, intellectual development from the concrete to the more abstract, and social and emotional changes. As they move from childhood to adolescence, they begin to see themselves and the world around them in different ways. The social studies curriculum for these students is critical because students begin to form their own values, life views, and modes of living, and begin to come to grips with the many complexities of adolescence and adulthood. The development of a positive self-concept is critical because strong peer pressure is a major influence in their lives, but a positive self-concept is developed only through accomplishments. They need to develop a healthy respect for others in our rapidly changing pluralistic world (Carnegie Council on Adolescent Development, 1989).

> *The development of a positive self-concept is critical because strong peer pressure is a major influence in their lives, but a positive self-concept is developed only through accomplishments.*

It is important that the social studies curriculum include topics that engage students' interest as well as extend their context for learning to different regions of the earth to gain a global perspective. Students can begin to understand situations from other perspectives and recognize the right of others to express differing points of view. Learning activities should be varied because of the sometimes short attention span of students; they should include both physical and social movement and involvement, such as role-playing and simulations; and they should involve both inquiry and didactic teaching and learning.

It is also useful to integrate social studies content with art, music, literature, science, mathematics, and environmental studies. Interdisciplinary content and multiteam teaching are commonplace in these grades. A variety of media can serve as sources of both motivation and information, helping students make connections between their world of here and now and the rest of the world.

Viewing the World from Different Perspectives (Grades 6–8)	
Theme	***Content Theme Questions***
Culture	What is culture? How are cultural regions similar and how are they different? What are some issues, crises, and opportunities facing each culture region at present? How might they be resolved?
Time, Continuity, and Change	How have leaders shaped the course of history? How have the common people contributed to our well-being? What roles have women played in the creation and development of our nation?
People, Places, and Environments	What is the nature of the earth and its environment today? What does it mean to call the earth our home? How do people make the earth their home? How will we protect space?
Individual Development and Identity	How does the perception we have of ourselves as individuals and as a nation influence the way we behave toward one another?
Individuals, Groups, and Institutions	What efforts are made to recognize and appreciate cultural diversity and unity in our country?
Power, Authority, and Governance	What legal rights and responsibilities do individuals and groups in our country and in other countries have?
Production, Distribution, and Consumption	How have world regions become increasingly specialized in the production and distribution of certain goods, thereby forming systems of economic networks?
Science, Technology, and Society	How have science and technology influenced our lifestyles, values, and expectations? How might technology shape our lives in the twenty-first century? How have technological developments changed the lives of people around the world? How has technology changed the ways persons and nations view the world and respond to events?
Global Connections	How might world peace be achieved within and among the cultures of the world?
Civic Ideals and Practices	What common challenges are faced by people around the world? How are they likely to respond to these challenges to ensure our survival on earth?

High School Students (Grades 9–12)

Social studies in grades 9–12 should include the opportunity to study in depth (1) our national heritage in a global setting through the study of history, economics, and government; (2) other nations, cultures, and environments; and (3) other social science disciplines through synoptic, behavioral, or analytic studies. Ideally, students will be required to take a social studies course during each of their years in high school and have the opportunity for instruction in at least one course that focuses on synoptic, behavioral, and analytic studies. Examples of social studies course offerings appear in Figure 3.

Examples of Social Studies Course Offerings		
Synoptic Studies	*Behavioral Studies*	*Analytic Studies*
Cultural/Global Studies	Anthropology	Economics
Humanities	Community/Civic Work	Environmental Issues
Philosophy	Futuristic Studies	Law-Related Education
Religious Studies	Ethnic Studies	Political Science/Government
Science, Technology, and Society	Human Development	Social Mathematics
World Geography	Sociology	
History (United States, World, and Regional)	Psychology	
	Social Issues of Teenage Life	
	Women's Studies	

Figure 3

Social studies instruction should include both descriptive and procedural knowledge of the several social sciences disciplines. Critical and creative thinking and problem-solving activities should be emphasized to enable students to gather and weigh data from several sources, to make judgments, and to formulate conclusions. Teachers need to pose questions that will promote genuine classroom discussion and allow for the development of inductive, deductive, analogic, and evaluative thinking skills.

Classroom methodology needs to be varied to account for different learning styles, abilities, talents, and interests of the students. High school students should be provided with opportunities to develop and apply previously learned academic and social-participation skills to new content by examining critical issues in detail from different perspectives. Active learning is encouraged, as is direct involvement in the community through such activities as community or civic work, surveying people on important issues, or volunteering to work for a political candidate. A wide range of instructional materials (including electronic databases) available for student and teacher reference will encourage learning to learn and promote lifelong education.

Studying the World in Depth	
Theme	**Theme Content Questions (Grades 9–12)**
Culture	How do the cultures of various Western and non-Western societies contribute to our understanding of the world today?
Time, Continuity, and Change	Why have there been tensions and conflicts between and among various minority groups in the United States and elsewhere around the world? How have rising expectations of minority groups brought about change? What challenges remain to be resolved?
People, Places, and Environments	What will our planet Earth be like in the coming years and decades?
Individual Development and Identity	How can we achieve peace within ourselves? How can we help others achieve peace?
Individuals, Groups, and Institutions	How have changes in societies' expectations, values, and lifestyles influenced the role of women and the opportunities available to women at present and in coming years?
Power, Authority, and Governance	How have civil liberties been gained, and how are they protected?
Production, Distribution, and Consumption	How do people create wealth, participate actively in economic and political processes, and make decisions to ensure economic, social, and political justice?
Science, Technology, and Society	What major scientific discoveries and technological inventions have occurred in the United States and elsewhere in the world during the past 50 years? What effects have these changes had on us as individuals, as a nation, and as members of the global community of humankind?
Global Connections	What political, humanitarian, economic, and moral roles do international organizations play in various global settings?
Civic Ideals and Practices	How can citizens serve their schools and the larger community? What is the good citizen? What is the good person? What is the good society?

Content Course Requirements in the 6–12 Program

    While the authors do not suggest a specific sequence of courses for the 6–12 social studies curriculum, we do recommend a requirement that at least two years be devoted to the study of the United States, two years devoted to the study of the world, and three years devoted to the study of several social science disciplines (including the behavioral sciences), with an emphasis on civics and economics. Within this structure, four years of attention should be given to United States history and world history/geography within a global context. A curriculum committee could design a number of sequence patterns that would rely on the strengths of the teaching staff. For example, the curriculum committee might develop a pattern in which a one-year course in geography is followed by a two-year sequence in world history (to include attention to the political and philosophical ideas upon which our republic is built), or a three-year program in which students can expand their civic development and social conscience and gain a firm foundation in the cultural values of United States democracy. Within these last three years, special attention would be given to the study of political, economic, and behavioral science content and their application to local, state, national, and global issues and policies. The design possibilities are almost endless. Of more importance, however, is the *integrity of the content* (standards) that make up these sequence designs.

> Note: Much of this chapter has been adapted from Michael Hartoonian and Margaret Laughlin, "Designing a Scope and Sequence in Social Studies for the 21st Century," *Social Education*, Vol. 53, No. 6, (October), 388–398, 1989; and *Expectations of Excellence: Curriculum Standards for Social Studies*, Bulletin 89. Washington, DC, National Council for the Social Studies, 1994. Used with the permission of the National Council for the Social Studies.

Reference

Carnegie Foundation. *Turning Points. Preparing American Youth for the 21st Century.* New York: Carnegie Foundation, 1989.

Chapter 3

Assessing Student Learning in Social Studies

I am persuaded there is among the mass of people a fund of wisdom, integrity, and humanity . . .

—John Adams (1777)

Few would disagree that assessing student learning is essential to effective teaching and student growth and requires careful and thoughtful attention. Assessment influences student learning and helps teachers make more informed decisions. Interest in student assessment is growing, as students must be able to apply what they have learned to real-world settings, work with others to solve pressing social problems, and be willing to explore new ideas and develop new skills. Assessment has received widespread attention since President George Bush, as a part of the America 2000 strategy, announced the need for achievement tests covering the "core subjects" in which students would demonstrate competencies in mathematics, science, English, history, and geography based on "new world-class standards." Goals 2000 legislation, the Educate America Act, was signed into law by President Bill Clinton on March 31, 1994. Students in grades 4, 8, and 12 are expected to demonstrate competencies in English, mathematics, science, foreign languages, civics, government, economics, arts, history, and geography (Goals 2000: Educate America Act, 1994). Many believe national tests, such as those proposed, would motivate students to achieve, schools to improve, colleges to make better admission selections, and employers to make sound employment decisions. A demand for teacher and district accountability for student performance is increasing in many communities.

Until fairly recently, most districts used standardized norm-referenced tests to assess student learning. In general, whole-class administered, standardized, objective multiple-choice or fill-in-the-blank test questions require a memorization of facts and view learning as a product. These tests have been constructed for broad applicability rather than for a specific curriculum. Most standardized tests require students to choose a single correct answer and do not encourage multifaceted thinking. More recently, some tests now include writing samples of student work.

Various states have constructed or developed their own state assessment instruments, similar in scope and format to the existing national tests. Students' scores on these off-the-shelf tests are reported usually once a year to students and parents. The test results are communicated by the media—often with unfair comparisons among students, teachers, schools, districts, and states. It is important to keep in mind that most standardized tests are constructed and scored to discriminate among student test takers.

Traditional tests do not report what students think about, the context in which they are learning, or how they think about their learning; neither do they reveal the learning strategies students use to make sense of the world, nor how students verify and/or revise their thinking, nor whether students have accepted ownership for their learning (Church, 1991). Clearly, teaching and learning must be congruent with assessment and evaluation.

At present, educators, parents, business leaders, and policymakers are beginning to understand that assessments of student learning have broader implications for curriculum content, teaching methods, selection of instructional materials, and professional development. Assessment results are also used to develop district or school practices and, by policymakers, to develop educational policies that are intended to promote quality teaching and learning. As society changes, there are increasing demands for students to complete complex tasks that require higher-level thinking and communication skills for personal and social decision making.

States, districts, and classrooms are currently in the process of considering the use of performance assessments that may be either process oriented, such as defending a point of view about a controversial issue, or product directed, such as creating a replica of a medieval castle. Without doubt, performance assessment is a very complex way to determine student learning. Until now, assessments were used most often in creative activities, such as the arts, journalism, photography, and modeling (Winograd and Gaskins, 1992), where judgments are subjective.

In addition, many states and districts are requiring multiple assessments of student learning in several content areas, most often in grades 4, 8, and 10 or 12, which may be viewed as a culmination of school efforts and student learning. It is assumed that content assessed at these grades will have been taught in earlier grades. Thus, large-scale, few-response items, which can be machine scored and from which information about the test-taking population can be extrapolated at a minimum cost, are being reconsidered. Such assessments provide a snapshot of student information at a single point in time.

> In reality, classroom assessment is an almost continuous process. It involves observations, professional judgment, and interactions with students (discussions and conversations), while gathering various types of information about individual students.

Current Trends In Classroom Assessment

Salvia and Ysseldyke (1995) indicate that there are three major concerns about assessment. First is the overreliance on norm-referenced achievement tests that provide one dimension of student achievement at a particular point in time. Second is the confusion about what can and should be assessed. Third is an overreliance on objective and quantifiable measures for data collection.

Alternative assessments differ from conventional pencil-and-paper tests and may include authentic assessment, performance-based assessment, portfolios, exhibitions, observations, oral conversations, demonstrations, journals, and self-assessment. These and other forms of assessment require young learners to construct meaning by engaging in active learning in their development of critical-thinking skills.

Grant Wiggins (1993) coined the term *authentic assessment* to describe performance-based, realistic, and instructionally appropriate assessment. These practices are integrated into classroom instruction. They include what students should know and what they should be able to accomplish within a range of tasks. In performing such tasks, students are expected to apply higher-level thinking skills and problem-solving abilities to situations that are needed in the larger community. Wiggins noted that standards should be measurable, should indicate a specific level of performance, and should be high and out of reach for most students. The scoring criteria, guidelines, or rubrics are written to reflect the specific behaviors that are to be exhibited to meet the particular standard. Standards and the criteria communicate teacher expectations to students, parents, and the local community.

> Options for student assessment have been prompted by curriculum reform based on the development of national standards in the social studies and several social science disciplines, contemporary research findings related to classroom instructional practices, student interest and learning, and student and teacher accountability.

The following terms are often used interchangeably in the literature. In this publication the terms are defined as follows.

Assessment

is a process for obtaining, synthesizing, and interpreting information to measure student growth and development, to make decisions about students, and to meet state or district evaluation needs. The process presumes breadth of information and includes the use of multiple strategies and procedures in many settings and over various time periods. Ideally, assessment includes observations of daily work, performance samples that reflect student accomplishments (such as the ability to draw a mental map or construct a model), and tests to check on learning. Also, students face an ongoing assessment by peers, based on personal qualities, friendships, popularity, and the like.

Authentic assessment

is an examination of a student's ability to use what has been learned to perform a task (or operation) that is similar to one that may be encountered in real-world settings. For example, students are asked to plan, construct, communicate, and explain their reasoning about a possible solution to a local political, social, or economic problem, such as whether to build a local convention center and sports arena in the community.

Evaluation

is the making of value judgments about the quality of the performance task. Such judgments are open to interpretation concerning student progress. Evaluation includes careful reflection and decision making about curriculum and instruction—delicate and difficult processes which are never totally objective. Evaluation is based on decisions about quality.

Measurement

is a systematic process of quantifying or assigning numbers to a particular performance, thereby differentiating the quality of student learning. Both formal (quantitative) and informal (observation) processes may be used to measure student learning. Measurement includes administering and scoring a test, while evaluation offers a judgment about the meaning of the reported test scores.

Performance-based assessment

enables the teacher to observe and make a judgment about a student's demonstration in creating a product, emphasizing the ability to use prior knowledge and skills to produce the individual work. Students may be asked to create a television or radio commercial or to design an advertisement introducing a new product.

Scoring Criteria, Rubrics, and Procedures

After students have completed the designated tasks, their performances must be evaluated based on established criteria, rubrics, and procedures.

Criteria   are narrative descriptions of a performance. Once criteria have been identified, a numerical scale or descriptive term is used to evaluate the level of performance. The criteria distinguish proficient from nonproficient performances.

Rubrics   use descriptors such as *advanced proficient, proficient, minimal proficient,* and *not proficient* to indicate the level of performance accomplished by the student. Of course, other descriptive terms may also be used to describe the performance accurately.

Scoring   may be either holistic or analytical and must focus on the important aspects of the performance. Holistic scoring is a single score based on the overall performance. Analytical scoring rates each dimension of the performance task separately and provides stronger diagnostic information. Whatever scoring method is used, scoring is neither simple nor straightforward. All scores must be interpreted.

> While there is no clear-cut indicator as to who should set standards—teachers, students, or both—there is agreement that standards should be made public.

Assessment Activities

Ten suggestions for alternative ways to assess student learning, other than objective standardized or teacher-designed tests, are described in the following pages. Any of the methods may be used in assessing student learning and all have relevance to the social studies standards. They complement each other and create a whole or more complete assessment of student learning. Of course, other ways to assess student learning in social studies are also possible.

1. **Portfolios** are used to highlight student work over time by including a well-organized collection of student work samples; interest inventories; self-evaluations; products, such as reports, poems, drawings, and photographs; examples of programs developed and presented; computer projects; audio- or videocassettes and tapes; and school awards and recognitions. By inference, portfolios are useful in deciding what a student is capable of accomplishing.

Portfolio assessment is the emerging type of alternative assessment and is integrated with instruction in many districts. Conferences between students and teachers are often integral to portfolio assessment, as the conferences tend to focus on student strengths and the need for self-improvement rather than on comparisons between students or on student weaknesses. Some teachers have decided it is better not to score the portfolio, but use it as a tool to provide feedback to students. Teachers will need to decide if there is sufficient time, expertise, and commitment to require and use portfolio assessment effectively.

Portfolio assessments are both process oriented and product directed. While there is no agreement concerning the contents of portfolios, teachers generally agree that they should be tailored for a specific purpose and that a great deal is required of them if portfolios are to have meaning for students, parents, and teachers. Most teachers would agree that students should help to decide what information and materials should be included in their portfolios, as students are responsible for their own learning. Often portfolios include products involving the cognitive domain, such as classroom assignments, reports, essays, and other written work (including rough drafts). Equally important are outcomes that involve the affective domain—attitudes, values, self-concepts, relationships, and motivations. Teacher observations, checklists, self-reporting by students, and peer relations are examples of materials that assess students in the affective domain.

The construction of a portfolio by students helps them gain insight about their own learning. Three types of portfolios seem to be emerging:

(a) **Showcase portfolio**, which includes samples of the student's best work.

(b) **Documentation portfolio**, a scrapbook that includes a variety of work samples.

(c) **Evaluation portfolio**, used mainly to access learning rather than a portfolio for instructional purposes. To be effective, portfolio assessment must (1) have a clear purpose; (2) have developed appropriate performance criteria; (3) have established a suitable context for learning; and (4) include reasonable scoring criteria (Airasian, 1997).

If a school decides to use portfolio assessment, several staff development days for thoughtful discussion and reflection will be needed. Topics for consideration should include—at a minimum—a discussion about assessment design, a decision about standards to be used, a consensus on standards for the portfolio review, a determination about the use of the portfolio, a provision for time to review portfolios, and how best to communicate the results by the portfolio review. An often-asked question by many teachers is "How do I grade a portfolio so that I can assign a letter or number grade?" There is no clear answer.

2. <u>**Journals, diaries, and learning logs**</u> allow students to enhance their understanding of social studies by keeping track of their progress during a specific time period or topic under study.

(a) **Journals** are usually loosely structured and allow students to have freedom to write what they wish. For example, in a response journal, students may write about their reaction to a specific historical event, such as the assassination of Martin Luther King, Jr.

(b) **Diaries** enable students to write about feelings and emotions, which they may or may not share with their teachers or others. Diaries may also include ideas for future study or enable students to try out new ideas for reflection. Students thus are able to share their perceptions, insights, and information by applying their reasoning skills. Teachers are likely to respond to student journals and diaries and thereby establish a dynamic interaction.

(c) **Learning logs** allow students to respond to information they have acquired from various sources—books, media, and personal experiences—on an agreed-upon topic or issue. Students may describe their achievements, indicate areas of difficulty, or describe experiences of success. A goal related to the use of learning logs is to have students reflect, analyze, describe, and make judgments about their personal learning experiences. Some authors may use the terms learning logs, response logs, and reading logs interchangeably.

3. **Cooperative learning** assessment encourages cooperative group work to achieve a common goal or objective. While cooperative learning groups may differ in organization and structure, most will be heterogeneous: Students of varying abilities will work together and learn from each other, for example, by assuming roles in the simulation of a city council meeting. The outcomes should be assessed based on contributions by groups of students and on individual student effort within the group or alone.

Often members of cooperative groups discuss and rate each other's performances. This process enables students to review and judge the performances of their peers, which may be used as a model to judge one's own work based on the same criteria.

4. **Individual research projects** allow students to study a topic in some depth for an extended period of time. Such a project enables students to use and develop a range of important social studies skills: gathering, organizing, and interpreting information from several sources; considering multiple perspectives; and communicating information to others in oral or written form, including the use of illustrations.

5. **Observation** is a traditional method of assessment commonly used in sports and music competitions, art and craft shows, and similar activities. However, rather than restricting their observations to students' products or performances, teachers could be asked to observe behaviors, such as practicing kindness to one another, effort and work in cooperative group settings, and so forth. They can note their observations of student behavior in journal or anecdotal accounts.

6. **Anecdotal records** are brief descriptive notes that are dated and written during or immediately after an observation—while the behavior or event is fresh in the teacher's mind. These records should provide sufficient detail so that the notes can be used at a later time. Notes may be recorded related to student behaviors, skills, interests, completion of assignments, and so forth.

7. **Student self-evaluations** enable students to reflect on and assess their own learning; they have far greater meaning for students who habitually assess their learning efforts conscientiously. Students may ask themselves questions such as "How well did I do on my sociology project?" "What did I learn about global interdependence when studying about the actions of the United Nations?" or "How can I improve my map skills as I study about Australia?" The use of self-evaluations encourages students to take responsibility for their learning by requiring them to assess their progress as learners.

8. **Checklists** usually include a written list of common observable traits to document information that requires little additional description. Checklists are diagnostic and provide a way to keep track over time of the acquisition of important social studies skills or content.

9. **Interviews**, sometimes called personal communication, may be used by teachers to gain insights into student learning. They often include open-ended reflective and nondirective questions that ask students about instructional practices, preferences, interests, attitudes, and so forth. If teachers use properly sequenced questions, information about students' reasoning processes is likely to become clear; questions can also be used to provide feedback related to student misconceptions or faulty reasoning.

    Teachers may also decide to use one or more of the following personal communication methods to help assess student learning:

    (a) **Instructional questions and answers** are used to promote student thinking and learning and to provide information about achievement.

    (b) **Conferences** provide opportunities for teachers and students to talk openly about student achievement, interests, lessons learned, and future plans for learning and other personal goals.

    (c) **Class discussions** allow teachers to listen to student interactions, judge the quality and effectiveness of student contributions, and make inferences about achievement.

    (d) **Oral examinations** enable students to provide oral responses and enable teachers and classmates to ask follow-up questions (Stiggins, 1997).

10. **Conversations** with others may provide insights which may otherwise be difficult for a teacher to generate on her/his own. If this form of assessment is used, it is important to secure reliable information from a person who is in a position to know about the achievement level of the student under discussion.

The real assessment of student learning takes place in the classroom on a daily basis. Care must be taken to provide quality instruction so that students will be able to meet or exceed performance expectations in social studies. Helping young learners develop competencies in the ten National Council for the Social Studies themes is a step in the right direction as teachers prepare students for effective citizenship roles and responsibilities in the twenty-first century.

Bibliography

Airasian, P. W. *Classroom Assessment.* 3rd ed. New York: McGraw-Hill Companies, 1997.

Church, C. J. "Record Keeping in Whole Language Classrooms" in *Assessment and Evaluation in Whole Language Programs.* 2nd ed. B. Harp, editor. Norwood, MA: Christopher-Gordon Publishers, Inc., pp. 177–200, 1991.

Salvia, J., and J.E. Ysseldyke, *Assessment.* 6th ed. Boston: Houghton-Mifflin, 1995.

Stiggins, R.J. *Student-Centered Classroom Assessment.* 2nd ed. Upper Saddle River, NJ: Prentice Hall, 1997.

United States Congress. *Goals 2000: Educate America Act.* Washington: Government Printing Office, 1994.

Wiggins, G. "Assessment: Authenticity, Context, and Validity." *Phi Delta Kappan*, Vol. 75, No. 3, pp. 200–214, December 1993.

Winogard, P., and R. Gaskins. "Improving the Assessment of Literacy: The Power of Portfolios." *Pennsylvania Reporter*, Vol. 23, No. 2, pp. 1–6. 1992.

Additional Readings

Johnson, N.J., and M. Rose. *Portfolios: Clarifying, Constructing, and Enhancing.* Lancaster, PA: Technomic Publishing Company, Inc., 1997.

McMillan, J.H. *Classroom Assessment: Principles and Practices for Effective Instruction.* Boston: Allyn and Bacon, 1997.

Chapter 4

Implementing Social Studies Standards in the Classroom

The primary purpose of social studies is to help young people develop the ability to make informed and reasoned decisions for the public good as citizens of a culturally diverse, democratic society in an interdependent world.

—National Council for the Social Studies, 1994

The standards developed by the National Council for the Social Studies reflect current thinking by classroom teachers, discipline scholars, and teacher educators about what it is that is important for young people to know about themselves and their community: local, state, national, and international. Today, more than ever, learning must extend beyond the past and the immediate here and now and consider the future. Today's learners will live, work, and play in the twenty-first century. They need to be prepared to meet the challenges of citizenship responsibilities, which extend beyond voting on Election Day to taking an active part in the community. It is recognized that younger voters are the least likely to cast a ballot in national or local elections. The social studies standards are viewed as a means to develop enlightened citizens who are able to make rational decisions based on evidence.

This chapter includes twenty illustrative examples of lessons/units of study that suggest ways for middle school and high school teachers to implement these standards. Of course, other valuable instructional lessons/units will be developed by creative teachers to meet specific local curriculum content requirements and the needs of learners enrolled in the local school and/or district.

The graphic organizer in Figure 4 on page 34 shows the focus of each lesson or unit at the middle school and high school levels for each of the ten standards. An examination of the graphic organizer indicates a range of topics that could be included in planning social studies lessons/units using the standards.

Each of the lessons/units identifies the overall social studies standard theme under study. The title identifies the content to be taught and is in the form of a fairly broad-based focus question to indicate a direction for the lesson. By using broad questions, which allow for multiple responses (divergent thinking), both students and teachers grapple intellectually with possible responses (however tentative) to these questions. While doing so, students and teachers together are engaging in inquiry and the construction of both personal and social knowledge.

Given that there are numerous social studies scope-and-sequence models in use, the suggested grade levels (6–8 in the middle school, 9–12 in the high school, or other variations) and length of time are general. Teachers should decide when and where the topic best fits their curriculum and how the amount of instructional time available for the lessons/units can be adapted to meet local needs.

An overview of the context setting for a specific lesson is important. For each of the lessons/units, a brief description is included to offer a perspective about the lesson.

The objectives for the lesson/unit are illustrative examples and certainly are not inclusive. Using the same or similar content, other objectives should be added, deleted, or revised. While most of the objectives are in the cognitive domain, they also ask students to develop information and use skills to make their learning meaningful.

Several examples of illustrative concepts and skills are suggested. Once again, these suggestions are not the only concepts and skills that could be developed for any of the lessons/units. Teachers are encouraged to identify and select concepts and skills that may have greater meaning for them and their students.

The learning procedures are suggested as one or more examples of how teachers may decide to present a specific theme. The lessons are some-what flexible. For example, the second learning activity for middle school students using the theme of culture suggests using artifacts from the Egyptian and Aztec cultures. If the study of these cultures is not included in the local curriculum, the same activity could be used when teaching about Greek and Roman cultures to accomplish similar objectives. Flexibility in choosing important content and valuable instructional strategies is one of the characteristics of quality social studies programs.

Several examples of ways beyond the traditional multiple-choice, fill-in-the-blanks, and true-false tests to evaluate student learning are suggested. The examples of student evaluation activities suggest ways students can use and apply what they have learned about the content, as well as ways they can develop and expand their skills. These examples of student evaluation activities are related to student performance and assessment, which are required in many districts and states.

> A word of caution is in order. Terms such as *evaluation, assessment, performance standards,* and *benchmarks* have multiple definitions, depending on the author or presenter. A clear definition and understanding of these terms and other jargon are encouraged to avoid undue confusion. It is recommended that teachers incorporate the terminology and vocabulary used in their states and districts.

Each activity suggests instructional materials for students and teachers. Many of these materials are general—specific titles of books and other instructional materials are not listed for each lesson. Most schools and communities are likely to have a range of available materials that address the suggested content and provide additional background materials for both students and teachers which should be utilized.

Before using the lessons/units, teachers should check on available resources with the school's media center, the department office, and the public library. When relying on the local library and/or interlibrary loan networks for access to materials, teachers should talk with library personnel in advance so they will be prepared when the young learners arrive to use the resources, including access to the Internet and various databases, which may not be available at school.

For some lessons, examples of specific instructional resources, such as video programs, are listed. These examples are suggestions for possible inclusion in the lessons/units. They may enhance the learning environment and recognize different learning styles. They are not necessarily an integral part of the particular lesson/unit. No attempt has been made to provide an extensive list of instructional/teaching materials. Many other titles and materials are available in local communities.

The Social Studies School Service has a wide range and extensive inventory of social studies instructional materials for various grade levels, subject content areas, and price ranges. Its inventory includes books, posters, videocassettes, reproducible masters, computer programs, games, and simulations. If you are not already familiar with this service, write to the company for a catalog of social studies materials available. Many professional organizations and associations also have instructional resources available for purchase.

As teachers reflect on content to be taught, teaching and evaluation strategies, and resources to be used, this book and its examples of the lessons/units to promote active learning should be helpful starting points.

Focus of Lessons/Units for Each Theme		
Theme	**Middle school**	**High school**
Culture	How do we learn about a culture? (Lesson 1–A)	What can we learn about a culture from its arts? (Lesson 1–B)
Time, Continuity, and Change	How do people record events and trends over time? (Lesson 2–A)	The search for democracy: Are global changes reshaping history? (Lesson 2–B)
People, Places, and Environments	How has geography contributed to the cultural diversity of Latin America? (Lesson 3–A)	How has the physical environment shaped the Russian and Eurasian republics? (Lesson 3–B)
Individual Development and Identity	How do social issues influence decision making? (Lesson 4–A)	Why do child abuse and neglect exist in a nation that claims it puts children first? (Lesson 4–B)
Individuals, Groups, and Institutions	Why is there violence in schools? (Lesson 5–A)	How is sociological research used? (Lesson 5–B)
Power, Authority, and Governance	What are some basic concepts of democracy? (Lesson 6–A)	Political influence and special interest groups: What are their roles in a democratic society? (Lesson 6–B)
Production, Distribution, and Consumption	What trade-offs are included in making any choice? (Lesson 7–A)	How is income created? distributed? (Lesson 7–B)
Science, Technology, and Society	How do discoveries in science and inventions in technology influence society? (Lesson 8–A)	How do science and technology interface with society? (Lesson 8–B)
Global Connections	How does my community or state connect with individuals, groups, and nations around the world? (Lesson 9–A)	What ethical, social, political, and economic forces influence the achievement of world peace? (Lesson 9–B)
Civic Ideals and Practices	Who should be included in a citizens hall of fame? (Lesson 10–A)	How do citizens influence campaign issues? other voters? (Lesson 10–B)

Figure 4

Organizational Structure of Lesson 1-A

THEME: Culture

TITLE OF LESSON/UNIT (TOPIC):
How Do We Learn About a Culture?

SUGGESTED GRADE LEVEL/LENGTH OF TIME FOR LESSON/UNIT:
middle school/two to five days or longer,
depending on depth of lesson/unit

Setting the Context for the Lesson/Unit

People in every culture and civilization leave behind material objects that were used in daily life. Such objects, called artifacts, could include coins, toys, clothes, cooking utensils, tools, weapons, furniture, jewelry, etc. Determining how these artifacts were used helps anthropologists and archaeologists understand a culture or civilization. As scientists examine the artifacts, they are able to suggest how people lived, their beliefs, their traditions, and so forth.

Objectives for the Lesson/Unit

Students will

- Study one or more artifacts (or pictures of artifacts) from a culture box created by the teacher and class or from a commercially prepared culture box with several examples of artifacts from a specific culture, such as Inca, Tibetan, etc.

- Decide what is already known about the culture under study

- Pose questions to elicit additional information about the culture under study

- Seek answers—or tentative answers—to the questions posed

- Offer generalizations about the lifestyle and/or quality of life of the culture under study

Illustrative Examples of Concepts

artifacts	culture
anthropologists	civilization
archaeologists	

Illustrative Examples of Skills to Be Developed/Expanded

observing	hypothesizing
interpreting	formulating generalizations
drawing conclusions	

Procedures for Learning Activity(ies)

Divide the class into small groups. Ask students to examine each artifact, or picture of an artifact, carefully. Ask them to describe the object. Ask them to consider the following: where/when the object was found, how it might have been used, why it was used in that way, the materials used to create the artifact, etc. Then ask students to brainstorm important features of the culture based on an examination of the artifact or picture. What conclusions could they formulate about the culture under study, based on the evidence available, as they reflect on already known characteristics of the culture?

Or

Divide the class into two groups, or involve two classes in this project. For example, at the beginning of the school year have one class (group) study Egyptian culture in some depth and the other class (group) study Aztec culture in some depth. Ask the students to make artifacts representative of "their" culture and bury the artifacts in the school yard until spring. Then, in the spring, have students from the opposite class (group) "dig up" the artifacts of the "other" culture and respond to questions such as those posed in the above activity. Of course, students should not exchange information about "their" culture until after the "spring dig." At the end of the "dig," a modest "banquet" could be planned: students would eat foods representative of each culture and would report their findings. Parents and community members could be invited to participate in the "banquet" and hear the presentations. Of course, other culture groups could be included, and more than two classes or groups could engage in this activity.

Or

Ask students to build a culture box that contains objects which the students have brought from home. Each student should bring at least one object that is reflective of today's culture. Among the objects brought to class, students should reach agreement in deciding which ten to fifteen such objects should be included in their culture box. Students should decide which objects are most significant to them and why these objects represent their culture in the late 1990's. The students should identify the criteria used to include a particular object as an artifact. Why is it that one may be unable to examine a culture adequately by studying only artifacts of a culture?

Student Evaluation

Ask students to identify at least three artifacts found in their bedroom at home—clothes, technology objects, photographs, jewelry, makeup, etc. Then ask students to pretend they are anthropologists/archaeologists who uncover these objects 100 years from now. What would these artifacts suggest about the culture of the United States near the end of the twentieth century? What might future scientists write about United States culture at this time?

Or

Ask students to build a culture box that contains objects which the students have brought from home. Each student should bring at least one object that is reflective of today's culture. Among the objects brought to class, students should reach agreement in deciding which 10 to 15 such objects should be included in their culture box. Students should decide which objects are most significant to them and why these objects represent their culture in the late 1990's. The students should identify the criteria used to include a particular object as an artifact. Why is it that one may be unable to examine a culture adequately by studying only artifacts of a culture?

Materials/Data Sources Needed (Teacher/Students)

- Artifacts (original or models) or photographs of artifacts that reflect the culture under study
- Textbooks and other print and nonprint reference tools for use in examining one or more culture groups
- Materials, such as clay, wood, paint, glue, and tools to make artifacts reflective of the culture under study

CULTURE
Activity 1-A

How Do We Learn About a Culture?

People in every culture and civilization leave behind material objects that were used in daily life. Such objects, called **artifacts**, could include coins, toys, clothes, cooking utensils, tools, weapons, furniture, jewelry, etc. Determining how these artifacts were used helps anthropologists and archaeologists understand a culture or civilization. As scientists examine the artifacts, they are able to suggest how people lived, their beliefs, their traditions, and so forth.

1. Choose an artifact from the assortment in the culture box.

2. Examine the artifact closely. Describe the artifact.

_____

_____

3. When and where do you think the object was found? How do you know?

_____

_____

4. What materials were used to create the object?

_____

_____

5. How do you think the object was used?

_____

_____

_____

6. Why do you think the object was used that way?

_____

_____

_____

7. What does the object tell you about the culture we are studying?

_____

_____

_____

8. What do artifacts fail to tell us about a culture?

_____

CULTURE Evaluation 1-A

How Do We Learn About a Culture?

1. Identify at least **three artifacts** found in your bedroom at home. These artifacts could be clothes, technology objects, photographs, natural objects, or something else.

   _____

   _____

   _____

   _____

2. Imagine that you are an anthropologist/archaelogist who uncovers these objects 100 years from now. What would the objects suggest about United States culture of that "past" era?

   _____

   _____

   _____

   _____

3. What might future scientists write about the culture of the United States in the current era?

   _____

   _____

   _____

   _____

Culture Box

1. Bring from home one or more objects to include in a culture box that will be created by the class.

2. Examine the objects. Then identify 10 to 15 objects that should be included in the culture box. List these objects in the space below.

   _____

   _____

   _____

   _____

3. Explain why each of these objects should be included in the culture box. What criteria were used in making these decisions?

4. Why is it that one may be unable to examine a culture fully by studying only artifacts of a culture?

5. What other information would be useful in studying a particular culture?

Organizational Structure of Lesson 1-B

THEME: Culture

TITLE OF LESSON/UNIT (TOPIC):
What Can We Learn About a Culture from Its Arts?

SUGGESTED GRADE LEVEL/LENGTH OF TIME FOR LESSON/UNIT:
high school/several days, depending on depth of lesson/unit

Setting the Context for the Lesson/Unit

India's arts and crafts are among the finest and oldest in the world. They express a sense of unity as well as diversity. The arts reflect the rich cultural heritage of India. Until recently, Indian artisans, painters, sculptors, and architects used their talents to glorify rulers and gods as they decorated temples and public buildings. Today, the art of India is broadening its scope to reflect characteristics of a modern nation and reflect a blend of East and West.

Objectives for the Lesson/Unit

Students will

- Identify several influences related to the development of the visual arts (architecture, painting, and sculpture) in India

- Indicate ways in which traditional and modern visual and performing arts (music, dance, and theater) reflect Indian culture

- Recognize and appreciate the contributions the arts in India have made to other civilizations and nations

Illustrative Examples of Concepts

visual arts	performing arts
traditional arts	modern arts
stupas	sitar
mythology	minarets
expressive arts	music
films	dance

Procedures for Learning Activity(ies)

Ask students to read widely about the various traditional and modern arts (both visual and performing arts) in India. In small cooperative learning groups, students may focus on one of the arts, identify important characteristics of this art form, and report their findings to classmates. Students are then asked to create their own "Indian art" in whatever form they select. At the end of the unit, ask students to reflect on the influences the arts have not only in India, but elsewhere as well. Ask them to share the most interesting parts of the lesson with classmates.

Or

Ask student to compare a work of art from India (Asia), such as *Siva Who Bears the Crescent Moon*, with a work of art from another culture, such as *Nail Figue* from the Congo (Africa). Other expressions of art could be used for this activity, for example, compare the Taj Mahal with one of the great cathedrals of Europe, such as St. Peter's in Rome (architecture), or India's decorative cloth with that of Egypt.

Or

Ask students to view an Indian (Asian) film such as *Pather Panchali* or *The Companion of the Heart Is the Heart Itself* and compare these films (or others that are available) with those produced in Hollywood. The film industry in India is one of the largest in the world, producing over 800 films a year, which exceeds the number produced by Hollywood. Why is this the case? What kinds of films are produced in India? What is the average cost of a ticket to see a film in India? To what extent are Indian films available in the United States? Why or why not? What are the major themes of films produced in the United States? What are admission prices to see a film in the United States at first-run theaters? at second-run theaters? Why do ticket prices to attend films in India and in the United States differ?

Or

Ask students to listen to a recording of Indian music or view a film showing a folk dance from India. What is the historical and/or cultural content of the music or dance? Students should then seek answers to questions, such as the following: (1) Who is the composer? When was the music written? Why did the composer write the music? How was (is) the music performed? Who usually listens to the music? What is the role of music in India? In general, what can you conclude about music in India? (2) Who created the dance? Why and when was the dance created? To what extent is the dance performed today? What is the role of dance in India? (3) How do the performing arts reflect India's culture? What conclusions can you draw about the expressive arts in India?

Student Evaluation

Essay evaluations may ask students to respond to questions such as the following: (1) Explain how cultural influences have shaped the arts in India. (2) How have modern Indian art forms been influenced by traditional Indian art forms? (3) How are the arts in India a reflection of Indian unity? How do they reflect cultural diversity? (4) What are some beliefs, values, traditions, and interests that are often reflected in various Indian art forms? (5) How are the arts used for political purposes?

Or

Ask students to write a newspaper article describing the status of the arts in India in general for the travel section of a national United States newspaper.

Or

Ask students in a cooperative group to prepare a photo essay with captions and explanations that show characteristics of Indian art or artistic endeavors (values, interests, and beliefs) throughout the ages. The photo essay could be displayed in the media center, school hallways, or a local community mall displaying student efforts.

Materials/Data Sources Needed (Teacher/Students)

- Reference books and art books with examples of the arts of India and elsewhere
- Photographs of various images of Indian art
- Models or examples of various arts representing several of the arts in India—for example, architecture, literature, music, dance, theater, film, billboard announcements for the arts, radio, decorated cloth, masks, etc.

Illustrative Examples of Skills to Be Developed/Expanded

observing	searching
communicating	interpreting

Name _____   Date _____

What Can We Learn About a Culture from Its Arts?

India's arts and crafts are among the finest and oldest in the world. They express a sense of unity as well as diversity. The arts reflect the rich cultural heritage of India. Until recently, Indian artisans, painters, sculptors, and architects used their talents to glorify rulers and gods as they decorated temples and public buildings. Today, the art of India is broadening its scope to reflect characteristics of a modern nation and a blend of East and West.

1. Use a variety of books, the Internet, and other sources to become familiar with the art of India.

2. Think about which art form you would like to study: painting, sculpture, architecture, literature, music, dance, theater, film, cloth, etc. List your choices here and explain them briefly.

    First: _____

    Second: _____

    Third: _____

3. After your teacher assigns you to a group, meet with the other members to identify important characteristics of the art form selected. List them here.

    _____

    _____

    _____

    _____

4. As a group, prepare a report on your findings. Then try to create an example of your art form. Present the report and the example to the class on the date assigned by your teacher.

5. As a class, discuss the influences the arts of India have had on India itself and on other parts of the world. Write down some of your ideas here. What conclusions can you suggest?

    _____

    _____

    _____

    _____

6. What are some functions of the arts in any culture? Why are these important?

    _____

    _____

    _____

    _____

What Can We Learn About a Culture from Its Arts?

As a final step in this study of the art of India, you may choose to write either an **essay** answering one of the following questions or a **newspaper article**.

A. Essay

Write an essay on one of the following subjects or on a similar topic approved by your teacher.

- How have cultural influences shaped the arts in India?
- How have modern Indian art forms been influenced by traditional Indian art forms?
- How do the arts in India reflect Indian unity? Indian diversity?
- What are some beliefs, values, traditions, and interests that are reflected in Indian art forms?
- How are the arts used for political purposes?

B. Newspaper Article

Write a feature story for the travel section of a newspaper. The article should describe the status of the arts in India today.

Use the following space to make notes about your essay or article.

_____

_____

_____

_____

_____

_____

_____

_____

_____

_____

_____

Organizational Structure of Lesson 2-A

THEME: Time, Continuity, and Change

TITLE OF LESSON/UNIT (TOPIC):
How Do People Record Events and Trends Over Time?

SUGGESTED GRADE LEVEL/LENGTH OF TIME FOR LESSON/UNIT:
middle school/two to five days, with regular additions during the year

Setting the Context for the Lesson/Unit

Often students do not recognize that important and not so important events are taking place simultaneously around the world. While any time period could be selected for illustrative purposes, events on the international, national, state, and local levels will be suggested. Working with timelines is useful to help students gather, record, share, and summarize data from several sources, such as biographies, diaries, artifacts, eyewitness interviews, and other materials.

Objectives for the Lesson/Unit

Students will

- Identify world, national, state, and local events that took place during the decade of the 1980's for placement on a timeline

- Gather and organize data from several sources for placement on a timeline for the decade of the 1980's

- Examine the data recorded on the timelines and draw conclusions, however tentative, about events and/or conditions at each level of government

- Look for patterns of change and continuity during the decade of the 1980's and draw conclusions about the nature of these changes and continuity in society

- Speculate about possible events that might take place in the twenty-first century and place these speculations on timelines, using the same categories as above—namely local, state, national, and world events

Illustrative Examples of Concepts

time	timeline
continuity	change
chronology	decade
time interval	cause and effect

Illustrative Examples of Skills to Be Developed/Expanded

sequencing (organizing data)	formulating conclusions
identifying events	examining cause and effect
comparing data	

Procedures for Learning Activity(ies)

Prior to the lesson, prepare four large timelines for the decade of the 1980's. One time-line should be used to record world events, one to record national events, one to organize state events, and one to organize local events. One or two examples of events should be included on each timeline. After discussion and explanations, students should go to the library, refer to reference books and other instructional materials in the classroom, interview parents and others, and identify four to six other events that took place at each level during the decade of the 1980's (a total of 16 to 24 events should be on the four timelines). The events identified and their dates should be added to the correct timeline. Have the students comment about the events selected and their possible meaning for themselves and for others. Ask students to formulate one or more statements about the events recorded on their time-lines.

If space and time permit, create four "super timelines" for all to see. The super timelines could be placed on the walls. Ask students to record the data from their individual timelines on the appropriate super timeline. Have students examine the super timelines. Ask them whether having new information recorded on the timelines prompts them to change their earlier conclusions about the decade of the 1980's. Why or why not?

Student Evaluation

Ask students to name the decade of the 1980's (such as "Exciting Eighties" or "Time of Destiny") and give the reasons for their choice. Their reasons could be in the form of a picture, video, song, poem, or other creative endeavor, with explanations for their creation.

Or

Ask students to interview three or four people in the local community about what they remember of the decade of the 1980's. Prior to the interview students should prepare (with teacher guidance) questions to be asked of each person interviewed. Since it is difficult to record answers during an interview, two students might go together to an interview. One person asks the question and one person records the interview on a cassette tape recorder (with the permission of the interviewee). After the data are transcribed, a copy of the interview (questions and answers) should be verified for accuracy by the person interviewed. Students could complete a scrapbook with information (and pictures, if any) about the people interviewed for placement in the classroom or school library.

Materials/Data Sources Needed (Teacher/Students)

- Numerous references for research, including primary materials
- Copies of timelines for students to complete
- Sample timelines for explanation of task on overhead transparency
- Cassette recorders for oral interviews, if used
- Newsprint for super timelines, if constructed

Name _____ Date _____

How Do People Record Events and Trends Over Time?

LOCATION	YEAR	DECADE OF THE 1980'S								
	1980	1981	1982	1983	1984	1985	1986	1987	1988	1989
World										
National										
State										
Local										

LOCATION	YEAR	TIMELINE FOR THE 21ST CENTURY							
	2000	2010	2020	2030	2040	2050	2060	2070	
World									
National									
State									
Local									

TIME, CONTINUITY,
AND CHANGE
Evaluation 2-A

How Do People Record Events and Trends Over Time?

1. Think of an appropriate name for the decade of the 1980's.

     _____

2. Illustrate your choice of a name by drawing a picture, writing a song, composing a poem, or creating some way to express your knowledge of this decade and its meaning.

3. Interview several people in the community to find out what they particularly remember about the 1980's. Prepare questions in advance to ask.

4. Compile the answers from the interviews, include photographs and/or sketches, and add them to a class booklet about the decade of the 1980's.

5. Using an example of an event included on the timeline for the 1980's, explain how and why one of these events may be interpreted differently by various people, such as a participant in the event, a witness to the event, persons reporting the event, historians, and so forth.

Organizational Structure of Lesson 2-B

THEME: Time, Continuity, and Change

TITLE OF LESSON/UNIT (TOPIC):
The Search for Democracy: Are Global Changes Reshaping History?

SUGGESTED GRADE LEVEL/LENGTH OF TIME FOR LESSON/UNIT:
high school/several days, depending on depth of content coverage

---

Setting the Context for the Lesson/Unit

During the past half century, there have been many national and global trends or patterns that have emerged. In time, some of these recent and current trends and patterns may prove to be key turning points in history. They include the emergence of new independent nation states throughout the world; various economic and political reform efforts, in both developed and developing nations; revolutions in global transportation and communications, which have reshaped our communal identity; and struggles to improve the quality of life while trying to overcome numerous obstacles. All of these events may be viewed as turning points in history at a later date. It is too early to determine their long-term consequences and importance.

One major social change that has worldwide implications is the feminist movement. Women throughout the world are seeking to ensure social equality (in education, marriage, decision making, etc.), to secure political rights (the right to vote and participate in civic action), to gain economic opportunity (jobs and careers outside the home and family structure), and to realize a personal identity. These are fundamental human rights.

Objectives for the Lesson/Unit

Students will

- Examine how various political, social, economic, cultural, and religious forces have reshaped the lives of people, especially those of women around the globe

- Explain how social conditions and reforms have brought about changes in opportunities for women in different parts of the world historically and at present

- Analyze the political, social, and economic changes women have experienced in the past half century

- Evaluate the short-term and long-term consequences of the feminist movement from the perspectives of feminists and those who oppose feminism and the feminist movement

Illustrative Examples of Concepts

feminism	multiple causation
social change	civil rights
economic opportunity	human rights
personal identity	bias
social equality	quality of life
feminist movement	

Illustrative Examples of Skills to Be Developed/Expanded

analyzing	comparing
explaining	formulating questions
interpreting	gathering information

Procedures for Learning Activity(ies)

After a discussion of turning points in history, ask students to identify key events that have recently taken place or are now occurring around the world. Why may these events be considered turning points in history? Then ask students to identify several key turning points (both in the United States and around the world) that took place during the past half century. Why might historians and others consider these particular events to be important movements during this time period? How did these events help to shape or reshape history? Of the events identified, which would likely be considered significant in changing the contemporary world? Why?

Any of the events identified as significant could be studied in some depth in small groups or by individual students and shared with the class. Review the worldwide feminist (human rights) movement for study as a class. After discussing the feminist movement within the context of civil and human rights, have students identify forces and circumstances that gave rise to the feminist movement in the United States and elsewhere; analyze the major political, social, cultural, and economic issues involved as women have sought equity and equality of opportunity; review actions and reactions of individuals and organizations to the feminist movement; explore the changing goals/focus of the feminist movement and the issues dividing the movement; compare the feminist movement in the United States with similar movements (or nonmovements) around the world; and speculate on the short-term and long-term substantive consequences of this movement.

Student Evaluation

Ask students to assume they are writing an article about the feminist movement of the last half of the twentieth century for a news magazine in the year 2020. Their article should include information about the origins of goals of the movement, its accomplishments and failures, its leadership and opposition, and its subsequent outcome(s). The writer should conclude by offering a reasoned judgment about the overall effectiveness and consequence(s) of the movement.

Or

Bring together a collection of political cartoons or pictures (including videos), music, or pieces of literature (documents, stories, poems, etc.), and/or editorials that reflect some aspect of the feminist movement. Ask students to analyze these materials and indicate their effectiveness as a means of swaying public opinion about the goals and effectiveness of the feminist movement.

Materials/Data Sources Needed (Teacher/Students)

 A large collection of resource materials that reflect various perspectives on the movement—reference books, histories and narratives, pictures, films, videos, documents, congressional testimony, United Nations and other government documents, music, and public interviews of participants and observers.

<table>
<tr><td>

TIME, CONTINUITY,
AND CHANGE
Activity 2-B

</td><td>

The Search for Democracy:
Are Global Changes Reshaping History?

</td><td></td></tr>
</table>

During the past half century, there have been many national and global **trends** or **patterns** that have emerged. In time, some of these recent and current trends and patterns may prove to be key turning points in history. They include the emergence of new independent nation states throughout the world; various economic and political reform efforts, in both developed and developing nations; revolutions in global transportation and communications, which have reshaped our communal identity; and struggles to improve the quality of life while trying to overcome numerous obstacles. All may be viewed as turning points at a later date. It is too early to determine their long-term consequences and importance.

One major social change that has worldwide implications is the feminist movement. Women throughout the world are seeking to ensure social equality (in education, marriage, decision making, etc.), to secure political rights (the right to vote and participate in civic action), to gain economic opportunity (jobs and careers outside the home and family structure), and to realize a personal identity. These are fundamental human rights.

1. Identify several recent or current key events that, in time, may prove to be turning points in history.

_____

_____

2. Why might historians consider these events to be important movements?

_____

_____

3. Why do you think the events you listed have such significance?

_____

_____

4. How did these events help to shape or reshape history?

_____

_____

5. Choose one of the listed events to study. Make notes on the back of this sheet as you prepare a report on the event to present to the class.

6. Use the back of this sheet to make notes on the key events your teacher and classmates select for class discussion.

(continued)

| TIME, CONTINUITY, AND CHANGE Activity 2-B | The Search for Democracy: Are Global Changes Reshaping History? *(continued)* |

Look back at your notes from the class discussion of the feminist movement. Choose one of the following projects. Use the space provided to make notes.

A. Article

Imagine that you work for a news magazine in the year 2020. Write an article from that future perspective about the feminist movement of the last half of the twentieth century. Include information about the movement's origins, goals, accomplishments, failures, and outcomes. What was the overall effectiveness of the movement? Why?

_____

_____

_____

_____

_____

_____

B. Analysis

Collect a number of items that reflect some aspect of the feminist movement— articles, pictures, cartoons, stories, poems, songs, and so forth. Examine each one and decide how effective it is in influencing public opinion for or against the movement. Put your conclusions into a written summary as to the effectiveness of these items to sway public opinion.

_____

_____

_____

_____

_____

_____

_____

Organizational Structure of Lesson 3-A

THEME: People, Places, and Environments

TITLE OF LESSON/UNIT (TOPIC):
How Has Geography Contributed to the Cultural Diversity of Latin America?

SUGGESTED GRADE LEVEL/LENGTH OF TIME FOR LESSON/UNIT:
middle school/several days

Setting the Context for the Lesson/Unit

More than 70 percent of Latin America's ethnically diverse population lives in or around urban areas such as Mexico City, Buenos Aires, and São Paulo, which places a heavy stress on local political and economic resources available to the people living in the cities and in the countryside.

Objectives for the Lesson/Unit

Students will

- Recognize that the population of Latin America is diverse due to its mixed ethnic heritage
- Examine the density and distribution of the population of Latin America and explain the root causes and effects of these conditions
- Describe the influence of European empires on the settlement patterns and development of the various Latin American cultures

Illustrative Examples of Concepts

settlement patterns	population distribution
population density	ethnic heritage
urbanization	migration
culture	civilization weather/
land tenure	climate
soils	theory of migration

Illustrative Examples of Skills to Be Developed/Expanded

observing data
categorizing data
using various types of maps (political, climate, cultural, economic)

Procedures for Learning Activity(ies)

Place on the bulletin board a variety of pictures of people from several countries in Latin America engaged in various tasks and roles. A physical/political map of the region should be nearby.

Ask the students to speculate about the relationship between the work that people in the pictures are doing and the nature of the local economy. Then ask each student to write down three or four questions he or she would like to have answered as the class studies Latin American culture, lifestyles, quality of life, standard of living, and so forth.

Make copies of the questions for student use. You and your class may want to categorize the student-generated questions in some meaningful way. In cooperative groups, the students seek to find answers to the questions posed by members of the class. Students then complete a retrieval chart/spreadsheet based on information gathered through research.

In addition, students could be asked to assume the role of an economic adviser to offer possible solutions (through research and/or brainstorming) to the problem of overcrowding in the capital and other large cities within one of the Latin American or Caribbean nations. Have students identify factors that pull people to the city, as well as factors that push people from the countryside. Explain why people have a tendency to move from the rural areas (the contryside) to urban areas (cities).

In oral or written reports, with illustrated charts, maps, and graphs, students will share their learning about Latin America with classmates and others.

Student Evaluation

Ask students to create and write a postcard to a friend, indicating one or two characteristics they have learned about the relationship shared by the Latin American geography, its economy, and its lifestyles. The postcards (complete with illustrations) should be shared with classmates and posted on the bulletin board.

Or

The uneven distribution of diverse populations and developing economies is a problem not only in Latin America but elsewhere as well. Ask students to define the problem, to brainstorm possible solutions, to consider the obstacles involved, to offer suggestions to overcome the barriers they have identified, and to make suggestions to alleviate the problems. The solutions (however tentative) should be communicated in a report to government officials.

Or

Ask students to construct a new map of Latin America based on physical regions and determine how those regions coincide with the current political boundaries of Latin America. Or they could construct a new map of Latin America that more clearly represents the economic power of each Latin American nation. Students should explain in one or two paragraphs the shape of their newly created map and its importance in understanding Latin America.

Materials/Data Sources Needed (Teacher/Students)

- Numerous pictures of people of Latin America engaged in various tasks
- Physical/political maps of Latin America (and other maps—cultural, economic, resources, and religions, if available)
- Adequate school and/or public library references (print and nonprint materials)
- Access to various databases
- Newspaper and magazine articles related to the geography and people of Latin America
- Current geography and other social studies reference books

PEOPLE, PLACES, AND ENVIRONMENTS
Activity 3-A

How Has Geography Contributed to the Cultural Diversity of Latin America?

More than 70 percent of Latin America's ethnically diverse population lives in or around urban areas such as Mexico City, Buenos Aires, and São Paulo. This places a heavy stress on local political and economic resources available to the people living in the cities and in the countryside.

1. Examine the pictures on the bulletin board.

2. Think about the types of work the people in the pictures are doing in relation to the economy of the area. What are some of the occupations?

   _____

   _____

3. Write down three or more questions that you would like to find answers to as you study Latin American culture.

   _____

   _____

   _____

   _____

4. With other members of your cooperative group, look for answers to the questions you and your classmates asked. (Your teacher will distribute copies of the questions.) Also, try to suggest solutions to any problems you uncover.

   _____

   _____

   _____

   _____

5. Complete a chart or spreadsheet of your own creation based on your information.

6. As a group, put your information into the form of a report to the class, together with maps, graphs, and illustrations. Use the space provided to make notes.

   _____

   _____

   _____

   _____

Name _____ Date _____

How Has Geography Contributed to the Cultural Diversity of Latin America?

To complete your current study of Latin American culture, choose one of the following projects. Use the space provided here to make notes.

A. Postcard

Create a postcard that reflects what you have learned about Latin America. Then write the card to a friend. In your message, explain the relationship shared by the geography, economy, and lifestyle of the people.

_____

_____

B. Report

Research the problems Latin America faces because of its mixed population and its developing economy. Brainstorm some possible solutions to the problems you find. Write a report to government officials outlining the problems and offering your solutions to reduce or eliminate the problem(s).

_____

_____

C. Maps

Construct two new maps of Latin America.

1. Create your first map to show the various physical regions. Next mark the actual boundaries of the countries in dotted lines. Then note where the national, cultural, and physical boundaries coincide.

2. Draw your second map to show the economic power of each existing country. Then explain in a few paragraphs why the shapes on your map are unusual and how this representation is important in understanding Latin America.

D. Population Movement

The movement of people in Latin America and elsewhere is toward urban areas (cities). Develop a theory as to why people are drawn to cities.

(continued)

Name _____   Date _____

How Has Geography Contributed to the Cultural Diversity of Latin America?

(continued)

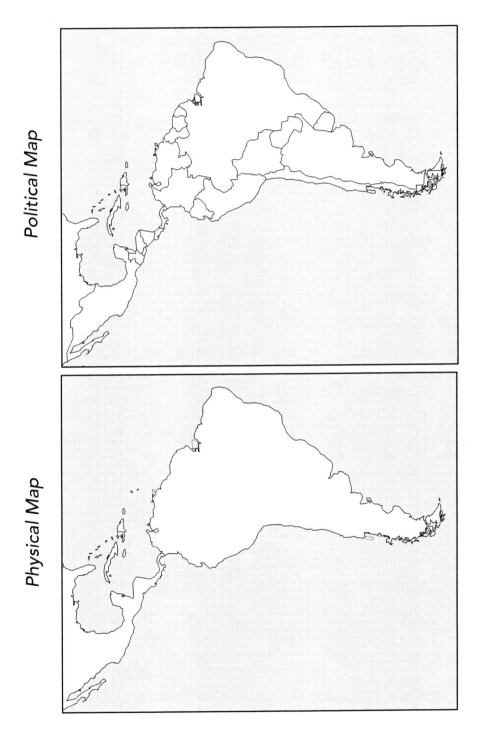

Political Map

Physical Map

Organizational Structure of Lesson 3-B

> THEME: People, Places, and Environments
>
> TITLE OF LESSON/UNIT (TOPIC):
> How Has the Physical Environment Shaped the Russian and
> Eurasian Republics?
>
> SUGGESTED GRADE LEVEL/LENGTH OF TIME FOR LESSON/UNIT:
> high school/several days

Setting the Context for the Lesson/Unit

The Russian and the Eurasian Republics extend halfway around the world and are larger geographically than the United States, Canada, and Mexico combined. Their vast size and northern location result in various landscapes and climatic zones which in turn have influenced the history, population patterns, cultures, and lifestyles of their people. Within the past decade, the former Soviet Union has experienced political and economic upheavals that affect not only this geographic region but other world regions as well.

Objectives for the Lesson/Unit

Students will

- Describe the major landforms of the Russian and Eurasian Republics
- Examine the significance of the major climatic regions included in Russia and the Eurasian Republics relative to population distribution of goods, and lifestyles
- Identify the diverse ethnic populations both historically and currently residing in Russia and the Eurasian Republics
- Indicate ways the various nationalities living in Russia and the Eurasian Republics express their national identities through culture
- Consider possible solutions (however tentative) to current environmental/political/economic issues which affect Russia and the Eurasian Republics

Illustrative Examples of Concepts

landforms	climatic regions
natural vegetation nation-	natural and human resources
alities	independence
cultural traditions	interdependence
nationality	ethnic populations

Illustrative Examples of Skills to Be Developed/Expanded

interpreting maps, charts, and graphs
gathering and interpreting data from many sources
locating specific geographic locations and/or regions

Procedures for Learning Activity(ies)

Provide a variety of maps and reference tools. Ask students to select a mineral or natural resource and indicate what types of industries could be developed in the area. What is the likely impact of these developments on the people and region? How would the industry be connected to the global marketplace? In developing this profile, consider other natural and human features, such as rivers, mountains, location, vegetation, and transportation systems.

Or

Ask students to create models of various Russian and Eurasian cultural symbols (for example, houses and religious buildings) or have students create a picture, poem, story, song, postage stamp, or paper money that reflects one aspect of the culture of a Russian or Eurasian Republic.

Or

Have students identify a Russian or Eurasian city of similar size to your city. Then have them prepare a report comparing the two cities and the surrounding regions.

Student Evaluation

Ask students to create a physical profile chart showing the major physical features of Russia and the Eurasian Republics extending from the Baltic Sea in the west to the Sea of Okhotsk in the east. Have students develop several bar graphs that show various aspects of Russia and the Eurasian Republics, such as population/population growth, imports/exports, climate, and so forth.

Or

This region of the world is experiencing many environmental problems such as population growth, nuclear energy, and the use of pesticides. Research one such issue and suggest policies which, if adopted, might help to diminish the problem.

Or

Have students collect the needed data from a variety of references and analyze the distribution of gods produced in Russia and/or the Eurasian Republics for export to their nations. In their research, students should consider the following questions: How have geographic location, climate, unequal distribution of resources, population settlement patterns, birth and death rates, cultural ethics and values, historic connections and traditions, and so forth helped to shape trade and economic interactions within and between these republics and the rest of the world? Students should then formulate a generalization about current trade patterns.

Materials/Data Sources Needed (Teacher/Students)

- Several political, physical, natural resource, population, and cultural region maps of Russia and the Eurasian Republics (both older and newer maps would be helpful)

- A variety of print and nonprint references

- A range of geography and social studies reference books that include data on the former Soviet Union and the Eurasian Republics

Name _____ Date _____

How Has the Physical Environment Shaped the Russian and Eurasian Republics?

    The Russian and the Eurasian Republics extend halfway around the world and are larger geographically than the United States, Canada, and Mexico combined. Their vast size and northern location result in various landscapes and climatic zones which in turn have influenced the history, population patterns, cultures, and lifestyles of their people. Within the past decade, the former Soviet Union has experienced political and economic upheavals that affect not only this geographic region but other world regions as well.

1. Identify three to five mineral or natural resources found in the Russian and/or Eurasian Republics.

    _____

2. What types of industries could be developed based on those resources?

    _____

    _____

3. What impact would the development of these industries have on the people and the environment of the area?

    _____

    _____

4. How might the industries be connected to the global marketplace? (Consider geographical features and transportation systems.)

    _____

    _____

Project

    Create one of the following cultural symbols that is in the style of, or reflects the culture of, the Russian and/or Eurasian Republics.

building	story	picture	paper money
postage stamp	song	poem	meal
cartoon	poster	diary	newspaper

Report

    Compare your city or town with one of similar size and latitude and continental location that is located in Russia or one of the Eurasian Republics.

PEOPLE, PLACES,
AND ENVIRONMENTS
Evaluation 3-B

How Has the Physical Environment Shaped the Russian and Eurasian Republics?

As a final project in your study of the Russian and Eurasian Republics, choose one of the following. Make notes in the space provided.

A. Chart

Create a profile chart showing the physical features of Russia and the Eurasian Republics. Cover the full expanse from the Baltic Sea in the west to the Sea of Okhotsk in the east. Then develop bar charts to graph population, climate, trade, and so forth.

_____

_____

_____

_____

_____

_____

_____

_____

_____

_____

B. Report

Research one of the region's problems, such as population, nuclear power, or pesticides. In a report, suggest policies (both short-term and long-term) that would help solve the problem.

_____

_____

_____

_____

_____

_____

_____

_____

_____

Organizational Structure of Lesson 4-A

THEME: Individual Development and Identity

TITLE OF LESSON/UNIT (TOPIC):
How Do Social Issues Influence Decision Making?

SUGGESTED GRADE LEVEL/LENGTH OF TIME FOR LESSON/UNIT:
middle school/five to ten days

Setting the Context for the Lesson/Unit

The office of the United States Surgeon General has provided strong warnings about smoking. Cigarette packages carry information about the harmful effects of smoking. Antismoking commercials appear in the media. Yet, a large number of young people begin or continue to smoke each year. Given the evidence linking smoking to health problems and other drug use, a comprehensive instructional unit using a variety of activities is appropriate for middle school students. The scare tactics used in the past to discourage smoking have not been effective. Currently there is a strong focus on self-esteem and decision-making skills. This unit is intended to help young learners study smoking and smoking-related issues as they decide whether to smoke, and to encourage them to consider the possible consequences of their decision. This unit could be expanded to include information about marijuana and alcohol prevention as well.

Consider the following questions: How do people decide to smoke or not to smoke? How are personal decisions influenced by social issues or social policies? How are decisions about smoking similar to other decisions made by adolescents and influenced by peer pressure? Is the incidence of smoking similar throughout the various states in the United States? throughout the world? Why might there be differences among those who choose to smoke and those who choose not to smoke?

Objectives for the Lesson/Unit

Students will

🌐 Identify ingredients in cigarettes that are harmful to their bodies

🌐 Give reasons why people smoke and why it is difficult to stop smoking

🌐 Explain the psychology cigarette advertisers use to encourage smoking, and identify ways cigarette advertisers target specific groups

🌐 Describe ways to refuse to begin smoking or ways to stop smoking

🌐 Consider the social implications of smoking on family (including infants), friends, tobacco producers, and businesses

Illustrative Examples of Concepts

personality	conformity
emotions	peer pressure
self-actualization	groups
heredity	groupthink
individual	family influence

Illustrative Examples of Skills to Be Developed/Expanded

identifying bias
organizing information
making decisions
forming personal opinions
communicating with various individuals and groups

Procedures for Learning Activity(ies)

1. Since the topic may be controversial in some communities, a newsletter or other communication prior to the beginning of the unit should be sent to parents and caregivers outlining the unit, topics to be addressed, resources to be used, homework assignments, etc. Such communication may be most valuable in encouraging parents to become involved in their children's learning.

2. Develop and conduct a survey to inquire about smoking use or nonuse for various age groups of people, such as elementary, middle and high school students; adults; cultural groups; females/males; and occupational groups.

3. Organize and interpret the collected data in a meaningful way and draw conclusions (however tentative) about smoking or non-smoking from the data.

4. Bring to class examples of cigarette advertising. Identify the intended audience, evaluate the economic persuasiveness of the advertisement and consumer response to the advertisement, describe the location and placement of cigarettes in stores, and so forth.

5. Ask students, in cooperative groups, questions such as the following: (a) Why does the United States government continue to subsidize tobacco farmers? (b) To what extent, if any, do the governments of other nations such as Japan, France, Austria, China, Canada, Mexico, and Egypt regulate smoking? (c) What are some private businesses that have regulations concerning smoking in the work/business environments?

6. Engage in role-playing in which students have opportunities to refuse to begin or continue smoking and to explain their reasons to their classmates.

Student Evaluation

Ask students to write an antismoking article (or editorial) for the school newspaper or for a newsletter to parents. As an alternative, have students create a TV or radio commercial, cartoon, story, or poem with an antismoking theme.

Or

Ask students to share information they have learned about smoking, including an antismoking provision with students in upper-elementary grades through skits, stories, music, and so on.

Materials/Data Sources Needed (Teacher/Students)

- Adler, T. "Infants' Deaths Become Less Mysterious," *Science News*, (March 11), p. 151, 1995.

- American Lung Association, Washington, DC

- Drug Education Center, Charlotte, NC

- Seachrist, L. "Nicotine Plays Deadly Role in Infant Death," *Science News*, (July 15), p. 39, 1995.

- Van de Kamp, J. "A New Solution to an Old Problem," *Schools and Drugs: A Guide to Drug and Alcohol Abuse Prevention Curricula and Programs.* Sacramento: Office of the California State Attorney General, 1987.

INDIVIDUAL DEVELOPMENT AND IDENTITY Activity 4-A

How Do Social Issues Influence Decision Making?

The office of the United States Surgeon General has provided strong warnings about smoking. Cigarette packages carry information about the harmful effects of smoking. Antismoking commercials appear in the media. Yet, a large number of young people begin or continue to smoke each year.

Survey

1. Develop a **questionnaire** to inquire about smoking and nonsmoking practices. Write out several questions you might ask.

_____

_____

_____

_____

2. Use the questionnaire to conduct a **survey** of various groups of people of all ages.

3. **Organize and interpret** the information you gather from the survey. Then draw some **conclusions** about the data obtained.

_____

_____

_____

_____

Ads

Collect cigarette advertisements from various sources. What segment of the population are they targeting?

To what extent do you think the ads are effective? Why or why not?

Role-play

With a partner, work up a skit in which you (1) decide that smoking is not for you and (2) explain your reasons. You may be able to perform the skit for younger children or at a parent-teacher program.

Name _____ Date _____

How Do Social Issues Influence
Decision Making?

Choose one of the following ways to express your anti-smoking ideas.
Make notes in the space provided.

A. An **article** for the school newspaper or parent newsletter

_____

_____

_____

_____

B. A **cartoon** or **comic strip**

_____

_____

_____

_____

C. A **story** for a younger student

_____

_____

_____

_____

D. A **poem** for your best friend

_____

_____

_____

_____

E. An **idea** of your own

_____

_____

_____

_____

Organizational Structure of Lesson 4-B

THEME: Individual Development and Identity

TITLE OF LESSON/UNIT (TOPIC):
Why Do Child Abuse and Neglect Exist in a Nation That Claims to Put Children First?

SUGGESTED GRADE LEVEL/LENGTH OF TIME FOR LESSON/UNIT:
high school/several days

Setting the Context for the Lesson/Unit

Child abuse, including physical or mental injury, sexual abuse, and psychological (emotional/verbal) neglect or mistreatment, is an ever-growing concern in our society. Daily, the incidents of abuse occur. While not all cases of abuse are reported, most people view abuse as a major social problem with over a million substantiated cases reported each year. Often, abusive parents and other adults were mistreated as children. Many adults have learned inappropriate ways to care for children. Therefore, they abuse their children by using harsh punishment. Others resort to violence due to stresses such as unemployment, ill health, divorce, or death. In addition, many abusive parents have unrealistically high expectations for children and/or are impatient with them. Parent education offered by the community, the establishment of parent support groups, and telephone hot lines are examples of programs that can help to reduce future violence and abuse.

Objectives for the Lesson/Unit

Students will

- Define child abuse and neglect as reflected in state statutes and other related documents
- Identify the root causes of child abuse and neglect
- Explain the responsibilities of various professionals such as medical personnel, educators, youth group leaders, and others to report suspected cases of child abuse to the proper authorities
- Locate and describe child support services available for prevention, intervention, and treatment in the local community
- Identify the characteristics of families and children at risk
- Read and discuss the United Nations Declaration on the Rights of Children as it relates to child abuse and neglect
- Suggest additional policies/procedures that may be helpful in reducing child abuse and neglect locally, statewide, nationally, and in the global community

Illustrative Examples of Concepts

child abuse	child neglect
violence	child mistreatment
physical/mental injury	stress
discipline	social service agencies
parental education	social/economic value

Illustrative Examples of Skills to Be Developed/Expanded

gathering, organizing, and interpreting data
solving problems
making decisions

Procedures for Learning Activity(ies)

1. Provide examples, and have students bring in examples of, child abuse situations as reported on TV and in magazines and newspapers. Provide copies of the reports for the class or place the information on a bulletin board.

2. Identify the environment in which the abuse took place and the characteristics of the offender.

3. Describe the role of the police and/or community service agency personnel. If possible, invite a person who works with cases of child abuse to come to the class to discuss child abuse locally. Students should have prepared questions in advance to ask the speaker.

4. Identify the legal action taken and the resolution of the cases under study.

5. Identify the major causes of child abuse. Group the reported abuses by category (females/males, age, type of abuse, etc.). Offer generalizations about the cases under study with respect to child abuse and neglect.

6. People are often neglected when they serve no function in our society. Until recently, young people had specific roles and responsibilities on family farms and in factories. Is it possible that children are abused and neglected because they add little economic value to the family, the family farm, or firm? What should a young person's role be in an information economy? What types of work should students engage in today? To what extent are young people viewed as a liability and burden or as an asset to the family unit? What is the real value of a child to our culture?

Student Evaluation

Having been presented with a case study related to child abuse and neglect (sample included, or substitute one written by the teacher), the student will write an editorial concerning the case and offer specific recommendations to reduce child abuse in general.

Or

Have students write a letter to the state bar association, urging guidelines for judges to use in sentencing child abusers.

Materials/Data Sources Needed (Teacher/Students)

- Numerous examples of articles dealing with child abuse or suspected cases of child abuse, and classic literature such as *Oliver Twist*, which describes child abuse, may be useful as well.

- Contact local community service and/or law enforcement agencies for a guest speaker who may bring to class various pamphlets and other printed information about child abuse and neglect.

- McEvoy, A. W. "Child Abuse Law and School Policy," *Education and Urban Society*. May, pp. 247–257, 1990.

- National Center for Educational Statistics. *Projections of Educational Statistics 1997–99*. Washington DC: Government Printing Office, 1991.

- National School Boards Association. *Violence in the Schools: How America's School Boards Are Safeguarding Our Children*. Alexandria, VA: National School Boards Association, 1993.

- In addition, teachers may want to contact the following organizations for information about child abuse.

National Center on Child Abuse and Neglect P. O. Box 1182 Washington, DC 20013	National Committee for the Prevention of Child Abuse 332 S. Michigan Avenue, Suite 1250 Chicago, IL 60604

Most states have various agencies or organizations that are likely to have information about child abuse and neglect in that particular state.

Example A—Child Abuse   Leslie was a nice-looking student who was new to the school in the fall. Leslie was quiet, reserved, and had made few friends. Leslie's grades were average. Even on hot days, Leslie wore long-sleeved shirts, avoided showering after gym classes, and sometimes came to school with unexplained bruises. During spring break, Leslie's battered body was found in a city several hundred miles away.

Example B—Child Abuse   Kim was a well-behaved child, a good student, outgoing, popular, and liked by teachers and students. Upon returning to school in the fall, however, Kim seemed to be a different person. Kim was now critical of others and verbally abusive to classmates and teachers. Kim's schoolwork was of poor quality. Kim's grades declined. Kim's parents were called to school for a conference.

> **Note:**   If students in the class have these names, be sure to change the names of the students in the examples. Gender neutral names have been used to avoid stereotyping behaviors and expectations.

Name _____   Date _____

Why Do Child Abuse and Neglect Exist in a Nation That Claims to Put Children First?

Child abuse, including physical or mental injury, sexual abuse, and psychological (emotional/verbal) neglect or mistreatment, is an ever-growing concern in our society. Daily, the incidents of abuse occur. While not all cases of abuse are reported, most people view abuse as a major social problem with over a million substantiated cases reported each year.

1. Bring in articles, news clippings, or other reports of child abuse cases.

2. As a class, group the abuse cases by category: type, gender, age, location, causes, results, etc.

3. What generalizations can you make about the causes of child abuse?

_____

_____

_____

_____

_____

_____

4. Describe the role that police and social service workers have in child abuse cases.

_____

_____

_____

_____

_____

5. What types of legal action occur in child abuse cases, and what is the outcome of such actions?

_____

_____

_____

_____

_____

<table>
<tr><td>

INDIVIDUAL DEVELOPMENT AND IDENTITY Evaluation 4-B

</td><td>

Why Do Child Abuse and Neglect Exist in a Nation That Claims to Put Children First?

</td></tr>
</table>

Read the following examples of child abuse or neglect. Based on your study of actual cases, offer some specific recommendations on how the abuse might have been avoided. Write your recommendations in the form of an editorial.

Example A—Child Abuse Leslie was a nice-looking student who was new to the school in the fall. Leslie was quiet, reserved, and had made few friends. Leslie's grades were average. Even on hot days, Leslie wore long-sleeved shirts, avoided showering after gym classes, and sometimes came to school with unexplained bruises. During spring break, Leslie's battered body was found in a city several hundred miles away.

Example B—Child Abuse Kim was a well-behaved child, a good student, outgoing, popular, and liked by teachers and students. Upon returning to school in the fall, however, Kim seemed to be a different person. Kim was now critical of others and verbally abusive to classmates and teachers. Kim's schoolwork was of poor quality. Kim's grades declined. Kim's parents were called to school for a conference.

_____

_____

_____

_____

_____

_____

_____

_____

_____

_____

_____

_____

_____

_____

Organizational Structure of Lesson 5-A

THEME: Individuals, Groups, and Institutions

TITLE OF LESSON/UNIT (TOPIC):
Why Is There Violence in Schools?

SUGGESTED GRADE LEVEL/LENGTH OF TIME FOR LESSON/UNIT:
middle school/several days

Setting the Context for the Lesson/Unit

The purpose of education is to transmit the cultural heritage of a nation from one generation to the next. In most societies, schools are the social institutions that have been given this responsibility. Today, numerous challenges confront schools. A study of school violence is appropriate for middle school students.

Objectives for the Lesson/Unit

Students will

- Describe the role of education in our society
- Differentiate between education and schooling
- Discuss causes and consequences of violence in schools
- Describe the relationship between violence and personal and social competence
- Propose solutions to help curb violence in schools

Illustrative Examples of Concepts

education	crime
schooling	mediation
violence	conflict resolution

Illustrative Examples of Skills to Be Developed/Expanded

gathering, analyzing, and interpreting data
defining terms
hypothesizing possible solutions
drawing conclusions

Procedures for Learning Activity(ies)

1. Ask students to define education and identify its purposes.

2. Ask students to define schools and school violence.

3. Ask students to provide examples of school violence in their own school or elsewhere.

4. Ask students to hypothesize about the causes of school violence and to identify consequences of school violence for students, families, the school, and the community.

5. Encourage students to examine one of the following hypotheses through social research: (a) that individual violence increases as levels of competition decrease or (b) that society will become more violent as its citizens are less competitive in work and family relations and in their role as citizens.*

6. Invite a police officer or community leader to discuss school violence in the community or local region. (Students should have several questions to ask the guest speaker prepared in advance.)

7. Ask students to suggest possible solutions (however tentative) to problems related to school violence.

Student Evaluation

Have students write a letter to the editor of the local paper urging a solution to school violence (in the local community, if applicable) or related to the larger problem of school violence in general.

Or

If school violence is a local school problem, have students present a report to the student council or the principal outlining specific steps that could be taken at the local school to reduce school violence; tell them to suggest possible consequences for such behaviors.

Or

Students could create their own posters for display throughout the school and/or write announcements to be read over the school public address system with ideas about how violence could be reduced or eliminated at the local school.

Or

Students could design a study to validate or invalidate the preceding hypotheses or another hypothesis that they generate themselves.

Materials/Data Sources Needed (Teacher/Students)

- A variety of newspaper/magazine articles or media reports related to school violence

- Invitation to a guest speaker—a police officer or community member who deals with school violence

- *Violence in Schools*, Cambridge. 10 posters. Available from Social Studies School Service, 10200 Jefferson Boulevard, Room 1421, P. O. Box 802, Culver City, CA 90232-0802, 1995

- Centers for Disease Control. *Youth Risk Behavior Survey.* Washington, DC: Government Printing Office, 1990.

---

* High school students may help middle school students research one of the hypotheses by examining the educational levels of those incarcerated; the relationship between students' tendency to cause trouble in schools and their overall grade point average; patterns of school attendance; and other social factors.

Name _____ Date _____

Why Is There Violence in Schools?

Violence is one of the most serious problems facing many schools today. School violence, a problem since the early 1960's, affects both teachers and students. In elementary schools, vandalism and extortion of younger students are common in some neighborhoods. Physical assaults against both students and teachers occur in high schools. The increase in violence is most prevalent in impoverished urban neighborhoods and schools where gangs exist. Sometimes gang members are school dropouts and do not allow nongang members to enter or leave the school. Drug sales and abuse take place on a regular basis. In addition, many hours of instructional time are lost due to bomb threats and false fire alarms. School property is destroyed, windows are broken, and books and materials are damaged by vandalism. Vandalism probably costs taxpayers over $600 million each year.

A recent Gallup poll found that 20 percent of Americans are concerned about the issue of discipline in the schools. As a matter of fact, polls conducted over the past two decades consistently have shown that the American people believe that lack of discipline is one of the chief problems affecting the nation's schools. Many educators believe there is a national epidemic of school violence.

The problem of school discipline is most apparent in the high number of assaults, rapes, and robberies that occur in American schools. Teachers increasingly are the victims of this violence. In Detroit, for example, student assaults against teachers rose 900 percent in a recent five-year period. In Cleveland, over 7,000 violent incidents against teachers were reported during one year.

Although no nationwide statistics exist to indicate whether school violence is on the rise, most experts agree that violent episodes increasingly involve deadly weapons. These attacks are likely to increase in the coming years. Few schools have been successful in combating violence for two reasons: (1) a lack of money and (2) a belief that there is no way to keep violence out of schools.

According to the Youth Risk Behavior Survey, conducted by the Centers for Disease Control, 20 percent of high school students carry a weapon at least once a month for self-protection or for use in a fight. One out of 20 high school students in the United States carries a firearm at least once a month. Thus, it is not surprising that shootings and hostage situations in school have occurred in at least 35 states around the nation. Furthermore, handgun homicides are now the second leading cause of death among high school students. Many students decide not to attend school because they are afraid and do not believe they are safe in school.

(continued)

       Succeed with the Standards in Your Social Studies Classroom

Why Is There Violence in Schools?

(continued)

To discourage students from carrying weapons, a growing number of schools are installing sophisticated security devices to help ensure student and teacher safety and to control access to and from the street. For instance, one fourth of the nation's large urban schools now use the handheld or walk-through metal detectors, most commonly seen in airports. In addition, about 245 of the nation's 15,000 school districts have their own police or security departments. In fact, New York City's school security force is the sixth largest police force of any kind in the United States.

Some educators believe that the best approach to curbing violence in schools lies in educational programs that teach young people how to resolve their disputes peacefully. The philosophy behind such programs is that young people who learn cooperation, concern for others, and problem-solving skills will be less likely to resort to violence. Thousands of schools across the nation, including elementary schools, now offer some kind of violence prevention program.

Some schools now offer intensive counseling services for students in trouble, while others have special programs to help students learn basic skills such as reading, writing, and mathematics. Schools also use codes for student suspension, student conduct, discipline, and cooperation with other social service/law enforcement agencies as measures to help reduce violent behaviors in schools.

1. Define **education**.

   _____

2. Identify the purpose(s) of education.

   _____

3. Identify and list several examples of school violence.

   _____

   _____

4. What are some of the consequences of school violence for those directly or indirectly involved?

   _____

   _____

5. Suggest some measures that you think might reduce the amount of violence in schools.

   _____

   _____

   _____

Name _____ Date _____

Why Is There Violence in Schools?

Select one of the following projects to complete. Use the space provided to make notes.

A. Research

Examine the following statements. Research one of them and prepare to discuss your findings in a debate with a classmate.

(1) Individual violence increases as levels of competition decrease.

(2) Society grows more violent as its citizens become less competitive at work, in family situations, and in the community.

_____

_____

_____

_____

_____

B. Letter

Write a letter to the editor of the local newspaper explaining why you believe it is crucial to solve the problem of school violence.

_____

_____

_____

_____

_____

C. Report

Develop a proposal for reducing violence in school. Prepare a report, outlining each step, and present it to the student council and school administration.

_____

_____

_____

_____

_____

Organizational Structure of Lesson 5-B

THEME: Individuals, Groups, and Institutions

TITLE OF LESSON/UNIT (TOPIC):
How Is Sociological Research Used to Influence Public Policy?

SUGGESTED GRADE LEVEL/LENGTH OF TIME FOR LESSON/UNIT:
high school/two or three days

Setting the Context for the Lesson/Unit

American sociologist C. Wright Mills calls for sociologists to apply the events of the real world to the daily life of individuals and groups. He suggests that members of society develop a sociological imagination, thereby allowing individuals to understand history, biography, and related events and to make connections between them as individuals and as the larger society. Making these connections is a characteristic of a social analyst, and it allows for the development of various perspectives. In his classic book *The Sociological Imagination*, Mills poses three broad categories of questions that lead to an understanding of society, its institutions, and forces.

The questions are

1. What is the unique nature of this particular society?

2. How has this society changed over time, and what are its unique characteristics in the historical period under study?

3. What types of people live in a particular society, and how do features of the society shape the human characteristics of its citizens?

A variety of other questions follow from these broad sociological questions.

Objectives for the Lesson/Unit

Students will

- Define sociology and a sociological perspective

- Explain the concept of a sociological imagination and its importance in analyzing the characteristics and qualities of a particular society

- Realize that behaviors are a blend or a result of the interactions of social influences and individual character

- Recognize the importance of viewing the world from several perspectives, and seek a balance of personal desires and the demands of others

Illustrative Examples of Concepts

sociology
sociological imagination
sociological perspective
sociological research
public policy

Illustrative Examples of Skills to Be Developed/Expanded

> defining terms
> analyzing data
> applying sociological concepts
> researching data from many sources

Procedures for Learning Activity(ies)

1. Ask students to define sociology and sociological perspective.

2. Introduce the concept of sociological imagination and discuss the fundamental questions Mills asks social analysts to consider.

3. Ask students to apply their sociological imaginations to a situation similar to the one that follows.

> You and several friends are attending a classmate's party to celebrate a sports championship at your school. You have been having a good time smoking and drinking alcoholic beverages. The alcoholic beverages have all been consumed. Scooter suggests driving over to another classmate's home to continue the party, since AJ's parents are gone for the weekend—and they always have a good supply of alcoholic beverages and snacks.

Consider and describe some social consequences of this scenario for the drinking students, other students not at the party, drivers, parents, members of the school championship team, law enforcement officials, and society at large. What conclusions can you draw from these behaviors?

Or

Consider this scenario as you think about social behaviors and their impact on social policies.

> You and several friends are frustrated by the few disruptive students in your high school. They are wasting precious classroom time and resources—and in some cases their misbehavior makes the school less safe for everyone. Several students from each class have been selected by the student government association to design a student behavior policy to alleviate this concern.

How would you research, prepare, and present your recommendations to the student body, the administration, the school board, and the community? How are your recommendations likely to be received and implemented in your school and in the larger community?

Student Evaluation

This will be a two-day evaluation activity.

Day 1 Evaluation   Ask students in cooperative groups of three or four to write a scenario that calls for students to express their sociological imaginations. Collect the new situations or scenarios for use in class the following day. You may need to edit the scenarios for consistency. Make copies of the scenarios available for each cooperative group on the following day.

Day 2 Evaluation   Distribute a different case study to each cooperative group. Ask the groups to exercise their sociological imaginations by analyzing the new scenario and discussing their thinking with the class. A transparency of each scenario would be useful so all members of the class can read the scenario being discussed by the cooperative group.

Materials/Data Sources Needed (Teacher/Students)

- Mills, C. Wright. *The Sociological Imagination.* (Copyright renewed 1987 by Yaralava Mills). London: Oxford University Press, 1959.

- A variety of sociology textbooks at the high school or university level and other related reference materials

- Overhead projector if transparency copies of the scenarios are to be viewed by the entire class during the discussion

Name _____ Date _____

How Is Sociological Research Used to Influence Public Policy?

American sociologist C. Wright Mills calls for sociologists to apply the events of the real world to the daily life of individuals and groups. He suggests that members of society develop a sociological imagination, thereby allowing individuals to understand history, biography, and related events and to make connections between them as individuals and as the larger society. Making these connections is a characteristic of a social analyst, and it allows for the development of various perspectives. In his classic book *The Sociological Imagination*, Mills poses three broad categories of questions that lead to an understanding of society, its institutions, and forces. The questions are: (1) What is the unique nature of this particular society? (2) How has this society changed over time, and what are its unique characteristics in the historical period under study? (3) What types of people live in a particular society, and how do features of the society shape the human characteristics of its citizens? A variety of other questions follow from these broad sociological questions.

1. Define *sociology*.

2. Participate in a group discussion of C. Wright Mills's concept of a *sociological imagination*. Then write a definition of sociological imagination, as you understand it.

_____

3. Apply your sociological imagination to the following situation.

> You and several friends are attending a classmate's party to celebrate a sports championship at your school. You have been having a good time smoking and drinking alcoholic beverages. The alcoholic beverages have all been consumed. Scooter suggests driving over to another classmate's home to continue the party, since AJ's parents are gone for the weekend—and they always have a good supply of alcoholic beverages and snacks.

What might be the consequences for individuals, parents, school, and community? Write your ideas on the back of this sheet.

4. Put yourself in the following situation.

> You and several friends are frustrated by the few disruptive students in your high school. They are wasting precious classroom time and resources—and in some cases their misbehavior makes the school less safe for everyone. Several students from each class have been selected by the student government association to design a student behavior policy to alleviate this concern.

How would you research, prepare, and present your recommendations to the student body, school officials, and the community? What would you report? Write your answer on the back of this sheet.

     Succeed with the Standards in Your Social Studies Classroom

INDIVIDUAL DEVELOPMENT
AND IDENTITY Evaluation
5-B

How Is Sociological Research Used to Influence Public Policy?

Day 1

With the other members of your group, make up a situation that calls for students to exercise their sociological imagination. Put the situation in writing. Edit as needed.

_____
_____
_____
_____
_____
_____
_____
_____
_____
_____

Day 2

Exchange written work with another group. Express your sociological imagination about the other group's situation. Then prepare your ideas for a class discussion on the new scenarios.

_____
_____
_____
_____
_____
_____
_____
_____
_____

Organizational Structure of Lesson 6-A

THEME: Power, Authority, and Governance

TITLE OF LESSON/UNIT (TOPIC):
What Are Some Basic Concepts of Democracy?

SUGGESTED GRADE LEVEL/LENGTH OF TIME FOR LESSON/UNIT:
middle school/several days

Setting the Context for the Lesson/Unit

Democracy exists in the United States because citizens believe in basic democratic values and concepts embedded in our political system. Our democracy will remain viable as long as these democratic beliefs and values continue: (1) the fundamental worth of each individual; (2) the equality of all people; (3) an ongoing belief in majority rule and minority rights; (4) the acceptance of compromise, as needed; (5) acting on the premise that individual liberty can be achieved only through civic responsibility; and (6) a belief in the rule of law. Government is the institution through which the people implement their values through public policy.

Objectives for the Lesson/Unit

Students will

🌐 Articulate the purpose of government in the United States

🌐 Recognize the basic rights and responsibilities of citizens and their participation in civic affairs

🌐 Explain the basic concepts of democracy as practiced in the United States

🌐 Describe the relationship of majority rule and minority rights in our democratic society

🌐 Explain the meaning of freedom, justice, and equality in the United States

Illustrative Examples of Concepts

democracy/democratic government	rule of law	compromise
	majority rule	civic responsibility
anarchy	public policies	minority rights
republic	social contract	citizen

Illustrative Examples of Skills to Be Developed/Expanded

analyzing information
formulating questions
reflective thinking
expressing oneself clearly
evaluating and influencing public policy

Procedures for Learning Activity(ies)

1. Ask students to describe the purpose(s) of government and how a government obtains and shares power and authority.

2. Ask students to review the basic principles of democracy as included in the Declaration of Independence, the United States Constitution, and other important historic documents, such as Supreme Court decisions.

3. Have students identify and explain the basic principles of democracy in the United States—individual rights; equality of opportunity; freedom of speech, press, and religion; right to assemble; majority rule, with protection of minority rights; responsibility for the common good; and equal protection under the law.

4. Ask students to give examples of these basic democratic principles and how they apply to them personally.

5. Ask students to consider how their lives would be different if these democratic principles were taken away and replaced by others.

6. The *Federalist Papers* suggests the fourth branch of government is "we the people." Ask students to explain their understanding of the meaning of the fourth branch of government.

Student Evaluation

Ask students to use the basic concepts of United States democracy that they identified to write at least two questions about each concept that they would like to have the president or congressional leaders answer.

Or

Have students, in small groups, write a basic document for the classroom which incorporates the basic principles and core values of our democracy.

Materials/Data Sources Needed (Teacher/Students)

- A variety of reference books and other printed materials

- Copies of the Declaration of Independence, the United States Constitution, the *Federalist Papers*, and other basic documents or statements about democracy in the United States

- Photographs from a range of sources in various time periods showing democratic principles in action

- Teachers may want to develop case scenarios involving basic principles of democracy in practice or violations of these principles—for example, a neighbor playing loud music that disturbs others in the neighborhood, a law enforcement officer stopping a bicyclist riding on the wrong side of the road and without a helmet, or other similar scenarios.

Name _____ Date _____

What Are Some Basic Concepts of Democracy?

Democracy exists in the United States because citizens believe in basic democratic values and concepts embedded in our political system. Our democracy will remain viable as long as these democratic beliefs and values continue: (1) the fundamental worth of each individual; (2) the equality of all people; (3) an ongoing belief in majority rule and minority rights; (4) the acceptance of compromise, as needed; (5) acting on the premise that individual liberty can be achieved only through civic responsibility; and (6) a belief in the rule of law. Government is the institution through which the people implement their values through public policy.

1. Describe the purpose of government.

   _____

   _____

2. How does a government obtain power and authority?

   _____

   _____

3. Identify and list some basic principles of democracy in the United States.

   _____

   _____

4. How do each of the democratic principles listed in question 3 apply to you?

   _____

   _____

   _____

5. How would your life be different without the democratic principles listed in question 3?

   _____

   _____

   _____

6. The *Federalist Papers* suggests that the fourth branch of government is "we the people." Explain your understanding of the fourth branch of government.

   _____

   _____

   _____

Name _____   Date _____

What Are Some Basic Concepts of Democracy?

Choose one of the following written projects. Use the space provided to make notes.

A. Write to the president or a congressional leader, asking some questions you have about the democratic principles you are studying.

_____

_____

_____

_____

_____

_____

_____

_____

B. As a group project, **write a document for the classroom** that contains the basic principles and core values of the nation's democracy.

_____

_____

_____

_____

_____

_____

_____

_____

C. What role should education play in the maintenance of our democracy?

_____

_____

_____

_____

_____

_____

_____

Organizational Structure of Lesson 6-B

THEME: Power, Authority, and Governance

TITLE OF LESSON/UNIT (TOPIC):
Political Influence and Special Interest Groups: What Are Their Roles in a
Democratic Society?

SUGGESTED GRADE LEVEL/LENGTH OF TIME FOR LESSON/UNIT:
high school/several days

Setting the Context for the Lesson/Unit

Political interest groups work extensively to influence public policy issues. They have several necessary and inevitable roles in the democratic political processes in the United States. They have their own special objectives. They seek to achieve their goals by applying pressure and making financial contributions to pressure policymakers.

Objectives for the Lesson/Unit

Students will

- Recognize that there is a range of interest groups reflecting the diverse interests of the people and that these groups enable people to express their interests and influence policy decisions

- Describe ways interest groups use their influence and resources to shape public opinion and public policy

- Examine ways in which citizens not attached to a special interest group can be represented in their state and federal government

- Explain the difference between power and authority

Illustrative Examples of Concepts

public policy	lobbying
public interest groups	fact/opinion
public opinion	pressure groups
propaganda/propaganda techniques	power
authority	

Illustrative Examples of Skills to Be Developed/Expanded

gathering and organizing data	interpreting data
defining and clarifying terms	

Procedures for Learning Activity(ies)

Ask students to complete Activity 6-B and discuss the influence of special interest groups in the most recent local, state, or national election. Ask the students to what extent the various interest groups influenced public opinion. To what extent did the amount of money available

to the interest group influence the shaping of public opinion and the outcome of
the election?

Students should interview people in the community who are members of special interest
groups and ask them about the function of the group, how the interviewee participates in the
group, the success the group has had in influencing the decision-making process, and so on.
These findings should be reported to the class. What was the impact, if any, of individuals who
were not a part of any group organized to influence voting behaviors?

Student Evaluation

Have students prepare a list of four or more questions on a current topic that an individual or a member of an interest group might address to a legislator or other government official. What group is being represented? How did the individual or group arrive at this group
position? How might the legislator respond to these questions?

Or

Tell students to assume that they are members of an interest group seeking to influence
Congress to pass laws allowing college students to receive tuition assistance of up to $15,000
per year for up to four years. In return, those receiving such assistance would have up to 50
percent of the total amount of the tuition assistance reduced in return for two years of public
service in various settings that would enable the college graduate to apply the information and
skills gained in college. What are the positive arguments for this legislation? How might critics
of this proposal respond? Have students develop an outline for influencing public policy on
this issue.

Or

Ask students to draft a bill or a resolution to be presented for consideration either by
Congress or by your state legislature; the bill should seek to regulate the political activities and
financial contributions from special interest groups or from individual voters. Who would
likely support this proposal? Who would likely be against it? Have students assess the likeli-
hood of passage of the bill or resolution at this point in time.

Materials/Data Sources Needed (Teachers/Students)

Examples of various materials related to special interest group activities/influences—
including headlines and news articles from the press, such as advertisements, feature arti-
cles/interviews, pamphlets, billboards, bumper stickers, T-shirts, hats, buttons/signs, etc.

<table>
<tr><td>POWER, AUTHORITY,
AND GOVERNANCE
Activity 6-B</td><td></td></tr>
</table>

POWER, AUTHORITY,
AND GOVERNANCE
Activity 6-B

Political Influence and Special Interest Groups: What Are Their Roles in a Democratic Society?

Political interest groups work extensively to influence public policy issues. They have several necessary and inevitable roles in the democratic political processes in the United States. They have their own special objectives. They seek to achieve their goals by applying pressure and making financial contributions to pressure policymakers.

1. Complete the following form by indicating the functions and criticisms of special interest groups as they exist today in the United States.

Functions of Special Interest Groups

_____

_____

_____

_____

_____

_____

Criticisms of Special Interest Groups

_____

_____

_____

_____

_____

_____

---

2. What conclusions can be drawn about the importance of special interest groups in the political processes?

3. To what extent do special interest groups represent the spirit of U.S. representative democracy? Why or why not?

POWER, AUTHORITY, AND GOVERNANCE
Evaluation 6-B

Political Influence and Special Interest Groups: What Are Their Roles in a Democratic Society?

Select one of the following projects to complete your study of special interest groups.

A. Current issue under discussion in your city, state, or nation

(1) Take a position on a current topic of importance to you.

_____

(2) (Imagine that you represent an interest group.) What interest group do you represent? Why are you representing the group?

_____

(3) Concerning your topic, list three or more questions to ask legislators or officials. After each question, offer a possible response.

_____

_____

_____

_____

B. Tuition

(1) Assume that you are a member of an interest group seeking to get laws passed for college tuition assistance—up to $15,000, half of which could be repaid by two years of appropriate public service.

(2) Present arguments for this legislation.

_____

_____

(3) Present arguments against this legislation.

_____

_____

(4) Develop an outline of a program for influencing public opinion on this issue.

_____

_____

_____

Organizational Structure of Lesson 7-A

THEME: Production, Distribution, and Consumption

TITLE OF LESSON/UNIT (TOPIC):
What Trade-offs Are Involved in Making Any Choice?

SUGGESTED GRADE LEVEL/LENGTH OF TIME FOR LESSON/UNIT:
middle school/two to three days

Setting the Context for the Lesson/Unit

Economics is concerned with human behavior and the choices that individuals and groups make in deciding how to create and distribute wealth and how to use scarce resources to satisfy human wants. On a daily basis, people make choices by considering the costs and anticipated benefits for each alternative choice.

Objectives for the Lesson/Unit

Students will

- Recognize that every individual or group choice has an opportunity cost
- Use the Problem-Solving Model (see Activity 7-A) to make a decision related to a real or a hypothetical problem
- Consider possible outcomes of their decision and decide which option to pursue

Illustrative Examples of Concepts

scarcity	alternative choices
criteria/judgment	opportunity cost
trade-offs	wealth

Illustrative Examples of Skills to Be Developed/Expanded

decision making
identifying the problem
identifying possible solutions
identifying, stating, and applying criteria for decision making
identifying and stating alternative choices for decision making

Procedures for Learning Activity(ies)

Provide students with a real or hypothetical situation requiring problem solving. For example, ask the class where they would like to go at the end of a school field trip, how to spend the $200 profit the class made from the recent pizza sale, or other similar economic decision-making activity.

Using an overhead transparency, ask the class as a whole to complete the problem-solving grid. Students should consider several possible alternatives and identify the criteria they would use to resolve the situation. Have them place a plus sign for agreement or a minus sign for disagreement (+ or −) in the grid space for each alternative based on the criteria. If there is no consensus, place a question mark (?) in the grid space. Ask students to explain the reasons for their choices.

Then give the students a second problem and ask them to work in small groups to complete a group decision-making grid and to explain their choices. It is possible that a group consensus may not be achieved, which is acceptable, as different students are likely to have different values and wants. Afterward ask students to discuss how their use of the decision-making process would be useful as they make personal decisions.

Student Evaluation

Ask students to make up a real or a hypothetical problem of their own and complete a new decision-making grid.

Or

Ask students to examine an economic issue facing the school or community and to use their decision-making skills to recommend a solution to the issue.

Or

Have students, individually or in small groups, create a budget for a family of four with an income of $35,000. They should decide the family's circumstances: source of income, housing, location and so forth. What dollar or percent of income should the family have available each month for items such as housing, food, insurance, medical, clothing, recreation, savings, utilities, taxes, transportation, and other goods and services? Students should share their budgets, and try to realistically assess their choices in allocating income. What adjustments, if any, are needed?

Materials/Data Sources Needed (Teacher/Students)

 Overhead projector

 Chalkboard/transparency of Activity 7-A for whole-class completion

PRODUCTION, DISTRIBUTION,
AND CONSUMPTION
Activity 7-A

What Trade-offs Are Involved in Making Any Choice?

Economics is concerned with human behavior and the choices that individuals and groups make in deciding how to use scarce resources to satisfy human wants. On a daily basis, people make choices by considering the costs and anticipated benefits for each alternative choice.

Problem-Solving Model: A Decision-Making Chart					
Problem: _____					
CRITERIA FOR MAKING A JUDGMENT					
Options/ Alternatives or Other Possible Choices					

1. What was decided?

2. What processes did you use in making your decision?

3. Was the decision the best possible choice? How do you know?

Name _____ Date _____

PRODUCTION, DISTRIBUTION,
AND CONSUMPTION
Evaluation 7-A

What Trade-offs Are Involved in Making Any Choice?

Select one of the following projects to complete your study of decision making.

A. Grid

1. Create a real or imaginary economic problem.

   _____

   _____

2. Construct a decision-making grid for working out the problem.

B. Economic Issue

1. Select a current economic problem facing your school or community.

   _____

   _____

2. Exercise the decision-making skills you have learned to suggest a solution to the problem.

   _____

   _____

3. What are some ways you can use a decision-making process in your daily life?

   _____

   _____

Organizational Structure of Lesson 7-B

THEME: Production, Distribution, and Consumption

TITLE OF LESSON/UNIT (TOPIC):
How Is Wealth Created and Distributed?

SUGGESTED GRADE LEVEL/LENGTH OF TIME FOR LESSON/UNIT:
high school/two to three days

Setting the Context for the Lesson/Unit

Personal income is the current income received from all sources minus the personal contributions to social insurance, such as Social Security and retirement. It includes transfer payments from government and business, such as Social Security benefits and public assistance, but excludes transfers among persons. The amount of personal income varies greatly in terms of geographic region, occupation, level of education, age, race, and gender. This lesson examines personal income distribution on a per capita, state-by-state basis. Perfect equality of income is rare and perhaps nonexistent.

Objectives for the Lesson/Unit

Students will

- Explain per capita income

- Define personal income, wealth, and social insurance

- Identify and analyze economic regions of the United States in terms of income distribution, and recognize that the amount of personal income varies among households and geographic regions

- Offer suggestions that help to explain variations in regional economic patterns

Illustrative Examples of Concepts

income distribution per capita	opportunities available
economic regions	personal income
current dollars	wealth
constant dollars	social insurance
productivity	infrastructure

Illustrative Examples of Skills to Be Developed/Expanded

organizing data
analyzing data
formulating hypotheses about changes in income distribution

Procedures for Learning Activity(ies)

Provide students with copies of Activity 7-B, which has the personal income per capita by states for 1980 to 1995 in both current and constant (1992) dollars. Ask the students to rank in order the income per capita for the years 1980 and 1995. (Number 1 is the state with the highest per capita income; 50 is the state with the lowest per capita income.) The ranking for each state should be written in the blank space as indicated. Then tell the students the top 12 per capita income states will be ranked in the top 25 percent; states between 13 and 25 will be ranked in the next 25 percent; states 26 to 38 will be ranked in the next 25 percent; and states 39 to 50 will be ranked in the bottom 25 percent. Ask the students to color code both U.S. maps (on page 95) by using green for the 12 states with the highest per capita income (states ranked 1 to 12); purple for the states ranked 13 to 25; yellow for the next 13 states (26 to 38); and blue for the bottom quarter of the states (39 to 50).

Ask students to indicate what patterns they notice by looking at the maps. Which regions have the highest income in 1980 and/or in 1995? What changes are there in the rankings of the states? Why might these changes have occurred? What are some causes for the unequal distribution of income? What other data would be helpful in studying about income distribution?

Student Evaluation

Ask students to explain what actions government (local, state, or federal), local businesses, and chambers of commerce might engage in to raise the personal income of workers in the states with the lowest per capita personal income. What are some pros and cons for such actions and/or policies for the following groups of people: business leaders, families, individual workers, social agencies, schools, the homeless, and the impoverished? What factors might account for change or a lack of change in income distribution?

Or

Have students compare their own state with other states in their own economic region and determine the economic circumstances that would allow for a growth of per capita personal income.

Materials/Data Sources Needed (Teacher/Students)

🌐 Several economics reference books to help explain economic concepts

🌐 Colored pencils, markers, or crayons

PRODUCTION, DISTRIBUTION, AND CONSUMPTION
Activity 7-B

How Is Wealth Created and Distributed?

Personal Income Per Capita
No. 699. Personal Income Per Capita in Current and Constant (1992) Dollars, by State: 1980 to 1995

REGION, DIVISION, AND STATE	CURRENT DOLLARS					CONSTANT (1992) DOLLARS					Income rank	
	1980	1990	1993	1994	1995	1980	1990	1993	1994	1995	1980	1995
United States	9,940	18,666	20,809	21,699	22,788	16,991	20,090	20,274	20,648	21,188		
Northeast	10,699	21,699	24,141	25,073	26,209	18,289	23,355	23,520	23,859	24,369		
New England	10,582	21,934	24,148	25,203	26,506	18,089	23,608	23,527	23,982	24,645		
Maine	8,218	17,039	18,687	19,481	20,527	14,048	18,339	18,206	18,537	19,086		
New Hampshire	9,803	20,227	22,312	23,679	25,151	16,757	21,771	21,738	22,532	23,385		
Vermont	8,546	17,442	19,394	20,100	20,927	14,609	18,773	18,895	19,126	19,458		
Massachusetts	10,659	22,247	24,410	25,608	26,994	18,221	23,945	13,782	24,368	25,099		
Rhode Island	9,576	19,032	21,231	21,948	23,310	16,369	20,484	20,685	20,885	21,674		
Connecticut	12,170	25,427	28,087	29,044	30,303	20,803	27,367	27,365	27,637	28,176		
Middle Atlantic	10,738	21,617	24,139	25,028	26,106	18,356	23,267	23,518	23,816	24,273		
New York	10.906	22,321	24,844	25,726	27,782	18,643	24,024	24,205	24,480	24,902		
New Jersey	11,648	24,182	26,834	27,741	28,858	19,911	26,027	26,144	26,397	26,832		
Pennsylvania	9,923	18,883	21,314	22,195	23,279	16,962	20,324	20,766	21,120	21,645		
Midwest	9,872	18,067	20,328	21,542	22,617	16,75	19,446	19,805	20,499	21,029		
East North Central	10,077	18,297	20,627	21,825	22,982	17,226	19,693	20,096	20,768	21,369		
Ohio	9,738	17,548	19,730	20,882	22,021	16,646	18,887	19,223	19,861	20,475		
Indiana	9,215	16,816	19,219	20,261	21,273	15,752	18,099	18,725	19,280	19,780		
Ilinois	10,875	20,159	22,533	23,607	24,763	18,590	21,697	21,953	22,464	23,025		
Michigan	10,154	18,237	20,599	22,172	23,551	17,357	19,629	20,069	21,908	21,898		
Wisconsin	9,772	17,398	19,824	20,887	21,839	16,705	18,726	19,314	19,875	20,306		
West North Central	9,374	17,520	19,619	20,870	21,753	16,024	18,856	19,114	19,859	20,226		
Minnesota	9,982	18,779	20,911	22,257	23,118	17,063	20,212	20,373	21,179	21,595		
Iowa	9,346	16,684	18,412	20,176	21,012	15,976	17,956	17,938	19,199	19,537		
Missouri	9,256	17,409	19,501	20,562	21,627	15,822	18,737	18,999	19,566	20,109		
North Dakota	7,641	15,321	17,212	18,610	18,883	13,062	16,490	16,769	17,608	17,353		
South Dakota	7,701	15,630	18,122	19,562	19,506	13,164	16,823	17,656	18,615	18,137		
Nebraska	8,988	17,379	19,693	20,819	21,703	15,364	18,705	19,186	19,811	20,179		
Kansas	9,829	17,642	19,880	20,762	21,825	16,802	18,988	19,369	19,756	20,293		
South	8,958	16,895	19,085	19,936	20,945	15,313	18,184	18,594	18,970	19,475		
South Atlantic	9,204	18,230	20,341	21,222	22,342	15,733	19,621	19,818	20,194	20,774		
Delaware	10,356	19,719	22,015	22,919	24,124	17,703	21,224	21,449	21,809	22,430		
Maryland	10,824	22,090	23,937	24,869	25,927	18,503	23,776	13,321	23,664	24,107		
District of Columbia	12,508	24,648	29,346	30,721	32,274	21,381	26,529	28,591	29,233	30,008		
Virginia	9,857	19,537	21,650	22,503	23,597	16,850	21,028	21,093	21,413	21,940		
West Virginia	7,972	13,967	16,230	17,089	17,915	13,627	15,033	15,813	16,261	16,657		
North Carolina	8,000	16,275	18,719	19,579	20,604	13,675	17,517	18,238	18,631	19,158		
South Carolina	7,558	15,106	16,877	17,713	18,788	12,920	16,259	16,443	16,855	17,479		
Georgia	8,353	17,123	19,244	20,198	21,278	14,279	18,430	18,749	19,220	19,784		
Florida	9,935	18,788	20,795	21,654	22,916	16,812	20,222	20,260	20,605	21,307		
East South Central	7,730	14,792	17,089	18,020	18,884	13,214	15,921	16,649	17,147	17,558		
Kentucky	8,051	14,747	16,887	17,752	18,612	13,762	15,872	16,453	16,892	17,305		
Tennessee	8,010	15,905	18,458	19,446	20,376	13,692	17,119	17,983	18,504	18,946		
Alabama	7,656	14,903	17,104	17,925	18,781	13,087	16,040	16,664	17,057	17,463		
Mississippi	6,868	12,571	14,713	15,791	16,531	11,740	13,530	14,335	15,026	15,371		
West South Central	9,329	15,908	18,151	18,906	19,816	15,947	17,122	17,634	17,990	18,425		
Arkansas	7,371	13,784	15,980	16,818	17,429	12,600	14,836	15,569	16,003	16,205		
Louisiana	8,672	14,281	16,555	17,615	18,827	14,824	15,371	16,129	16,762	17,505		
Oklahoma	9,308	15,119	17,041	17,602	18,152	15,911	16.273	16,603	16,759	16,878		
Texas	9,840	16,749	19,023	19,719	20,654	16,821	18,027	18,534	18,764	19,204		
West	10,889	19,296	21,036	21,629	22,852	18,614	20,768	20,495	20,581	21,248		
Mountain	9,455	16,589	18,975	19,789	20,900	16,162	17,855	18,487	18,831	19,433		
Montana	8,728	14,741	17,624	17,824	18,482	14,920	15,866	17,171	16,961	17,185		
Idaho	8,433	15,301	17,717	18,406	19,264	14,415	16,469	17,261	17,515	17,912		
Wyoming	11,356	16,902	19,850	20,377	21,321	19,412	18,192	19,339	19,390	19,824		
Colorado	10,616	18,814	21,560	22,320	23,449	18,147	20,250	21,005	21,239	21,803		
New Mexico	8,147	14,213	16,295	17,025	18,055	13,926	15,298	15,876	16,200	16,788		
Arizona	9,272	16,265	18,194	19,153	20,421	15,850	17,506	17,726	18,225	18,987		
Utah	7,942	14,060	16,354	17,171	18,223	13,576	15,133	15,933	16,339	16,944		
Nevada	11,559	20,254	22,727	23,817	25,013	19,759	21,800	22,142	22,663	13,257		
Pacific	11,403	20,240	21,774	22,301	23,581	19,492	21,785	21,214	21,221	21,926		
Washington	10,716	19,265	21,838	22,542	23,639	18,318	20,735	21,276	21,450	21,980		
Oregon	9,863	17,199	19,534	20,467	21,736	16,860	18,511	19,032	19,476	20,210		
California	11,681	20,654	21,893	22,353	23,699	19,968	22,230	21,330	21,270	22,035		
Alaska	13,692	20,881	22,887	23,431	24,182	23,405	22,474	22,298	22,296	22,484		
Hawaii	10,87784	20,906	23,566	24,043	24,738	18,417	22,501	22,960	22,878	23,001		

X Not applicable.   Source: U.S. Bureau of Economic Analysis, *Survey of Current Business*, May 1996 issue

(continued)

How Is Wealth Created
and Distributed? *(continued)*

1980

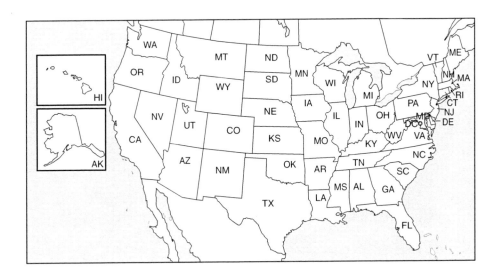

1995

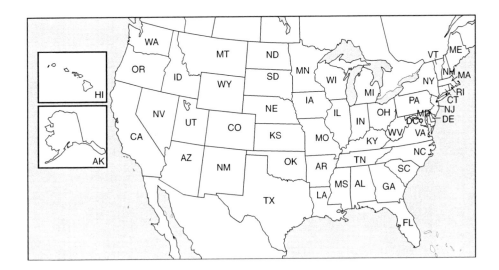

(continued)

Name _____ Date _____

How Is Wealth Created
and Distributed? *(continued)*

Personal income is the current income received from all sources minus the personal contributions to social insurance, such as Social Security and retirement. It includes transfer payments from government and business, such as Social Security benefits and public assistance, but excludes transfers among persons. The amount of personal income varies greatly in terms of geographic region, occupation, level of education, race, and gender.

Look at per capita income from the perspective of A or B.

A. Increasing Income Levels

1. What actions could governments and businesses take to increase the per capita income of workers in states at the bottom of the personal income range?

   _____

2. What effects would the actions listed above have on the following groups?

   (a) business leaders

   (b) families

   (c) individual workers

   (d) social agencies

   (e) schools

   (f) homeless

   (g) impoverished

3. What factors might account for change or a lack of change in income?

   _____

B. Comparing Income Levels

1. Compare the per capita income of your state with those of other states in your economic region. What conclusions can you make?

   _____

2. Determine the economic circumstances that would allow for growth of personal wealth.

   _____

Organizational Structure of Lesson 8-A

THEME: Science, Technology, and Society

TITLE OF LESSON/UNIT (TOPIC):
How Do Discoveries in Science and Inventions in Technology Influence Society?

SUGGESTED GRADE LEVEL/LENGTH OF TIME FOR LESSON/UNIT:
middle school/several days

Setting the Context for the Lesson/Unit

Throughout history people have made important scientific discoveries—the pull of gravity, the revolution of the earth around the sun, vaccines to eradicate or control diseases (polio, typhoid fever). People have also invented important technologies—the printing press, the gasoline engine, silicon chips, the heart pacemaker, home appliances, and others. Each day, in the United States alone, hundreds of new patents are issued based on new discoveries and/or inventions. Such discoveries and inventions affect the world's citizens and their environments for good or evil. It is important that citizens understand the ways that science, technology, and society influence one another.

For example, the automobile has shaped and been shaped by science, technology, and society. People view the automobile as both a positive and negative contributor to society. The pluses of the automobile include the ease of transportation for work, recreation, and family vacations; opportunities for the development of by-products and services; expanded new job possibilities; and much more. On the negative side, the misuse of the automobile has brought about accidents and deaths, pollution, traffic congestion of streets and highways, and more. A cost-benefit analysis is important to determine the overall value of such discoveries and inventions.

Objectives for the Lesson/Unit

Students will

- Identify and describe how science and technology have changed the lives of people and communities

- Identify scientists and inventors (both female and male) responsible for important discoveries in science and inventions in technology, and analyze their impact on society

- Explain how these developments changed people's perceptions of the world

- Suggest ways that individual values, beliefs, and attitudes may have been altered by the creation of new scientific and technological discoveries and inventions

- Predict possible new scientific discoveries and technological inventions that may become reality in the coming years

- Identify possible job opportunities in scientific and technological fields by examining job listings and their job-related qualifications in statewide and/or national newspapers

Illustrative Examples of Concepts

science	discovery
technology	cost-benefit analysis
biography	career choices
invention	society

Illustrative Examples of Skills to Be Developed/Expanded

decision making
researching
analyzing data
formulating generalizations

Procedures for Learning Activity(ies)

Students should:

1. Define the terms *science*, *technology*, and *society*.

2. Brainstorm historical examples of scientific discoveries and group these examples into meaningful categories (others can be added at a later time).

3. Write several generalizations about these examples of scientific discoveries.

4. Brainstorm historical examples of technological inventions and group these examples into meaningful categories (others can be added at a later time).

5. Write several generalizations about these examples of technological inventions.

6. Discuss similarities and differences based on these generalizations about scientific discoveries and technological inventions.

7. Select one of the historic discoveries or inventions identified above (or choose another) and prepare a research report on the discoverer or inventor for presentation to the class. (If available, use one of the "newer" technologies to prepare and present the report.)

8. Decide how these discoveries and inventions affected individuals and society at the time of their development and today.

9. Consider possible career opportunities in scientific and technical fields, and examine jobs currently available and likely to be available in the future in these areas.

Student Evaluation

Have students draw a sketch of a potential new technological invention or scientific discovery; then have them write a description of it and suggest its potential impact on society.

Or

Ask students to create a cartoon type comic strip showing several stages in the development of a discovery and/or invention, including society's response to this development.

Or

Tell students to create and prepare a personal application for a job in a scientific or technical field that currently exists or is likely to in the future.

Or

Have students identify and list several private and/or public problems, such as housing, transportation, pollution, etc., which need solutions. What new technologies and policies can help to resolve these problems?

Materials/Data Sources Needed (Teacher/Students)

- Numerous biographies/autobiographies of scientists and inventors
- Numerous reference books, magazines, and newspapers
- Sample job applications
- One or more speakers who are involved in science or technology to discuss work and career possibilities with the class
- *American Inventions.* Perfection Learning, 1991. (Six posters)
- *Change, Change.* CEL/BDM. (videocassette; 55 minutes; from *A Walk Through the 20th Century* series with Bill Moyers)
- *Famous Inventors Game.* HMS Historical Games.
- Sandler, Martin W. *Inventors: A Library of Congress Book.* New York: Harper Collins. (Hardback book)

(The latter four resources are available from Social Studies School Service, 10200 Jefferson Boulevard, Room 1421, P.O. Box 802, Culver City, CA 90232-0802.)

Name _____   Date _____

How Do Discoveries in Science and Inventions in Technology Influence Society?

Throughout history people have made important scientific discoveries—the pull of gravity, the revolution of the earth around the sun, vaccines to eradicate or control diseases (polio, typhoid fever). People have also invented important technologies—the printing press, the gasoline engine, silicon chips, the heart pacemaker, home appliances, and others. Each day, in the United States alone, hundreds of new patents are issued based on new discoveries and/or inventions. Such discoveries affect the world's citizens and their environments for good or evil. It is important that citizens understand the ways that science, technology, and society influence one another.

1. **Define** the following terms:

    (a) science _____

    (b) technology _____

    (c) society _____

2. **Brainstorm** several examples of **scientific discoveries**. Group them by category.

    _____

    _____

3. Offer some **generalizations** that apply to these discoveries.

    _____

    _____

4. **Brainstorm** several examples of **technological inventions**. Group them by category.

    _____

    _____

5. Offer some **generalizations** that apply to these inventions.

    _____

    _____

6. **Select** one discovery or invention. Research the person responsible for it. Prepare a report, using one of the newer technologies (if possible). Present the report to the class.

    _____

    _____

Name _____   Date _____

How Do Discoveries in Science and Inventions in Technology Influence Society?

Select one of the following projects to complete. Use the space provided here and on the back of this sheet to do a rough draft.

A. Sketch

Draw a sketch of an invention or discovery of your own. Then describe it and suggest its possible impact on society.

B. Comic Strip

Draw a comic strip showing the stages of development of a discovery or invention. Have the comic strip also show society's reaction to this development.

C. Job Application

Create an application for a job that you would like to have in a scientific or technical field that exists at present or could exist in the future.

D. Policies

At present there are numerous private and/or public problems in need of solutions. Identify and describe several such problems.

Think about one of the problems and indicate what technologies (either in current use or yet to be invented) might be helpful to solve the problem.

Then think about and identify existing policies that are intended to help find a solution to this problem. If existing policies are inadequate, develop a policy that might help solve the problem. Why might this policy be effective?

Organizational Structure of Lesson 8-B

THEME: Science, Technology, and Society

TITLE OF LESSON/UNIT (TOPIC):
How Do Science and Technology Interface with Society?

SUGGESTED GRADE LEVEL/LENGTH OF TIME FOR LESSON/UNIT:
high school/several days

Setting the Context for the Lesson/Unit

Scientific discoveries and technological inventions help individuals cope with the world in all sorts of ways—from the harnessing of energy for industrial production to home usage. Today's resources are limited, and an awareness of science and technology is essential, given the rapid rates of changes in demography, environmental destruction, governments, sustainable agriculture, transportation, communication, and so forth. A knowledge of the role of science and technology in a democratic society requires an informed electorate to make the best personal and social decisions and to take responsibility for those decisions. For example, consider how new discoveries such as cloning could affect our identity as human beings. Keep in mind that not every problem or concern cannot be resolved by science and/or technology alone, but that science and technology are important in resolving public policy issues.

Objectives for the Lesson/Unit

Students will

🌐 Recognize the impact of science and technology on society

🌐 Recognize the impact of society on science and technology

🌐 Give examples and explain how science and technology have impacted individuals and communities in the past and how they do so today

🌐 Gather information and take a stand on a current science and technology-related issue, for example, health care access; genetic engineering; illegal duplication of computer programs, videos, and tapes; and privacy of information in databases

Illustrative Examples of Concepts

science	urbanization
technology	ethical concerns
society	

Illustrative Examples of Skills to Be Developed/Expanded

identifying and researching examples of scientific and technological impacts
    on society
decision making
problem solving
developing an informal opinion on a policy issue

Procedures for Learning Activity(ies)

1. Ask students to write down several examples of what they know or think they know about scientific discoveries and technological innovations and to share these examples with the class.

2. Allow one to two days or more in the library for research. (Several days in advance, contact the local public library and notify the librarians of the project so that they can place appropriate materials on reserve to enable many students to have access to these references.)

3. Suggest that students record how various scientific discoveries and/or technological innovations impact their lives today.

4. Ask students to report their findings to the class in creative and innovative ways—role-playing, simulations, skits, etc.

5. Ask students to draw conclusions and make generalizations about scientific discoveries and/or technological innovations based on the data provided.

6. Ask students to explain how these generalizations apply to their community and/or state.

7. Ask students to examine the impact that pencils, ballpoint pens, office copy machines, and faxes have had on the modern office and businesses.

Student Evaluation

Ask students to design a new city and explain how technology is likely to impact the area as it is being created and developed. (Reston, Virginia, is an example.)

Or

Students could summarize the impact, both positive and less than positive, of a scientific discovery or technological innovation on the local community or region.

Or

Tell students to analyze the role of the U.S. Congress and/or state legislature in inhibiting or promoting the development of scientific discoveries—for example, BVG hormones to increase milk production—and/or technological innovations—for example, limiting young children's viewing of specific TV programs for the common good.

Or

Have students consider the following and prepare a statement supporting their position. If an individual has received an artificial heart or limb, to what extent is it appropriate to draw a clear distinction between a technological and a biological being?

Materials/Data Sources Needed (Teacher/Students)

- A variety of print and nonprint reference materials, including media clippings related to scientific discoveries and technological innovations

- American Association for the Advancement of Science. *Project 2061. Science for All Americans.* Washington, DC: American Association for the Advancement of Science, Inc., 1989.

- "The Agricultural Revolution: 8000 B.C.–5000 B.C." (Videocassette; 26 minutes; part of *The World: A Television History* series)

- Caselli, Giovanni. *History of Everyday Things: The Middle Ages* and *History of Everyday Things: The Renaissance and the New World.* Peter Bedrick.

"Industry and Empire: 1870–1914." (Videocassette; 26 minutes; part of *The World: A Television History* series)

"Science Technology and Man." New York Times. (Video from filmstrips; 29 minutes; part of the *Western Man and the Modern World* series)

The Scientific Revolution. (Hardback, part of *World History* series, 1994–1997.

"The Town." British Broadcasting Company. (Videocassette and guide; 20 minutes; part of *The Middle Ages* series)

(The above commercial materials are available from Social Studies School Service; 10200 Jefferson Boulevard, Room 1421, P.O. Box 802, Culver City, CA 90232-0802.)

SCIENCE, TECHNOLOGY, AND SOCIETY
Activity 8-B

How Do Science and Technology Interface with Society?

Scientific discoveries and technological inventions help individuals cope with the world in all sorts of ways—from the harnessing of energy for industrial production to home usage. Today's resources are limited, and an awareness of science and technology is essential, given the rapid rates of changes in demography, environmental destruction, governments, sustainable agriculture, transportation, communication, and so forth. A knowledge of the role of science and technology in a democratic society requires an informed electorate to make the best personal and social decisions and to take responsibility for those decisions. For example, consider how new discoveries such as cloning could affect our identity as human beings. Keep in mind that not every problem or concern can be resolved by science and/or technology alone, but that science and technology are important in resolving public policy issues.

1. Write down several examples of scientific discoveries and technological inventions.

   _____

   _____

2. Keep a record of how scientific discoveries and technological innovations impact your life during one day.

   _____

   _____

Before the development of technology, most people lived in small self-sufficient groups. They were hunters and gatherers who later became agriculturalists. During the Middle Ages in Europe, cities began to emerge. These early centers of population continued to expand. Today they are some of the great cities in Europe. Think about how the development of technologies helped bring about changes in these cities and contributed to the growth of cities in other parts of the world.

3. What technologies were involved in the development of urban areas?

   _____

4. To what extent did technology help meet human needs and transform society?

   _____

5. To what extent did technology help spread the wealth of a community?

   _____

6. To what extent did technology influence the opportunities for people living in your region?

   _____

SCIENCE, TECHNOLOGY,
AND SOCIETY
Evaluation 8-B

How Do Science and Technology Interface with Society?

Choose one of the following options. Use the back of this sheet to make notes.

A. City Design

Design a new city. Explain how technology is likely to impact the area as the city takes shape. Share your design with classmates and place your drawing or model in the media center.

B. Summary

Identify and summarize a technological development's positive and less than positive impact on the local community and region.

C. Government Restrictions

Analyze the role of the U.S. Congress or state legislature by inhibiting or promoting scientific developments.

D. Position Statement

Write a position statement in response to the following question. If an individual has received an artificial heart or limb, to what extent is it appropriate to draw a clear distinction between a technical and a biological being?

Organizational Structure of Lesson 9-A

THEME: Global Connections

TITLE OF LESSON/UNIT (TOPIC):
How Does My Community or State Connect with Individuals, Groups, and Nations Around the World?

SUGGESTED GRADE LEVEL/LENGTH OF TIME FOR LESSON/UNIT:
middle school/several days

Setting the Context for the Lesson/Unit

Events taking place around the world (terrorism, natural disasters, military conflicts, disease, and worldwide production of goods and services) affect individuals, communities, and nations in various ways. For example, modern means of transportation and communication—supersonic jets, media, and satellites; cultural exchange programs; international trade exchanges; and missionary activities—have linked the world, helping to create a global awareness in all of us. Global issues such as the extinction of endangered species, the depletion of natural resources, the depletion of the rain forest, whale fishing, managing world hunger, and protecting human rights have inspired both rhetoric and action and require both personal and social decision making.

Objectives for the Lesson/Unit

Students will

- Explain why many people believe the world is becoming more interconnected
- Identify historic and current global issues that affect society
- Suggest ways in which individuals, communities, and states can work together to solve ongoing and emerging global issues
- Initiate a pen pal connection with a person or classroom in another nation and begin to exchange information with one another via computer, personal contact, or the mail
- Explain why there is a greater need for local identity as the world becomes more connected globally
- Indicate ways the local community is linked to other communities around the world

Illustrative Examples of Concepts

global community	shrinking earth
international linkages	cooperation
interdependence	human rights
global awareness	

Illustrative Examples of Skills to Be Developed/Expanded

identifying cause and effect
decision making
gathering and analyzing information for informed decision making
examining alternative policies and points of view

Procedures for Learning Activity(ies)

1. Have students examine a world map, locate the local community and state and their relationship to other cities and nations around the world, and offer observations about these relationships.

2. Ask students to identify ways in which people and organizations in the local community and the state have established global connections, and suggest how these international connections could be expanded on a personal or community basis.

3. Have students identify and describe historic and contemporary global concerns that affect individuals and the community.

4. Have cooperative learning groups research background information for one of these concerns, and present the information to the class, including a cause-and-effect analysis.

5. Through class discussion, decide what action(s) could be taken by individuals, the community, and the state to help resolve these issues.

6. Let students explain how an individual can personally make a contribution (however small) to help ensure a better world.

7. As a class, work with civic, fraternal, religious, or other associations or organizations to develop an exchange program with young people in other nations—for example, a Sister City Program, an adopt-a-class project, or other similar programs.

Student Evaluation

Have students create a bulletin board collage using photographs, sketches, and narrative that indicate how individuals, the local community, and the state have global connections, and invite parents and community members to see the display.

Or

Let students prepare a video showing how individuals, the community, and state have connections to people in other nations, and show the video to various community groups, for example, business and civic organizations, senior citizens' groups, etc.

Materials/Data Sources Needed (Teacher/Students)

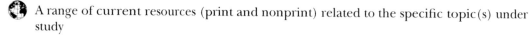 A range of current resources (print and nonprint) related to the specific topic(s) under study

Invite one or more qualified guest speakers to the class to discuss the topic(s) under study. Students should have prepared questions in advance of the presentation.

GLOBAL
CONNECTIONS
Activity 9-A

How Does My Community or State Connect with Individuals, Groups, and Nations Around the World?

Events taking place around the world (terrorism, natural disasters, military conflicts, disease, worldwide production of goods and services) affect individuals, communities, and nations in various ways. For example, modern means of transportation and communication—supersonic jets, media, and satellites; cultural exchange programs; international trade exchanges; and missionary activities—have linked the world, helping to create a global awareness in all of us. Global issues such as the extinction of endangered species, the depletion of natural resources, the depletion of the rain forest, whale fishing, managing world hunger, and protecting human rights have inspired both rhetoric and action and require both personal and social decision making.

1. Find your community and state on a world map. Think about the relationship of your location to other places around the world. Write down some of your observations.

   _____

   _____

2. Explain some ways in which your local community has global connections.
   Why are connections important?

   _____

   _____

   _____

3. Work with members of your group to examine a current global issue, research it, and prepare a presentation for the class.

   _____

   _____

   _____

4. What actions by you and/or your community could be taken to help resolve this issue?

   _____

   _____

   _____

5. Write a paragraph explaining how you as an individual can make a contribution to help ensure a better world.

   _____

   _____

Global
Connections
Evaluation 9-A

How Does My Community or State Connect with Individuals, Groups, and Nations Around the World?

Select one of the following projects. Use the space provided to make notes.

A. Bulletin Board

Create a bulletin board collage using photos, sketches, and narrative that explain how individuals, the community, and the state have global connections.

_____
_____
_____
_____
_____
_____
_____
_____
_____
_____

B. Video Presentation

Prepare a video or other visual presentation that shows how individuals, the community, and the state have connections to people in other nations.

_____
_____
_____
_____
_____
_____
_____
_____
_____
_____

Organizational Structure of Lesson 9-B

THEME: Global Connections

TITLE OF LESSON/UNIT (TOPIC):
What Ethical, Social, Political, and Economic Forces Influence the
Achievement of World Peace?

SUGGESTED GRADE LEVEL/LENGTH OF TIME FOR LESSON/UNIT:
high school/several days

Setting the Context for the Lesson/Unit

For most of our existence, humankind has not known peace. Internal and international conflicts have been ongoing throughout history. Virtually every generation of people has hoped for peace—preferably a lasting peace, which so far has remained elusive. Various individuals and organizations have sought to achieve peace through military action, signing international agreements to guarantee peace, issuing moral statements deploring violence, and offering to mediate disputes. For example, civil conflicts have erupted in recent years throughout the world: in Peru, China, India, Afghanistan, Central America, and elsewhere. International conflicts have occurred in Bosnia, Rwanda, the Persian Gulf, and the Middle East.

Relatively isolated incidents can have global impact. One example is the French government's decision to sink the *Rainbow Warrior*, the flagship of the environmental organization Greenpeace, when it was anchored in the harbor at Auckland, New Zealand. This violent act provoked much criticism throughout the world, grew into a major scandal within the French government, and damaged France's reputation worldwide. Another such incident was the sending of a submarine by North Korea to spy on South Korea. Later, under international pressure, North Korea issued a statement of apology. These two incidents had worldwide consequences. While the degree of actual bloodshed and hardship may vary, the result is the same: Peace does not exist.

Objectives for the Lesson/Unit

Students will

- Define peace and identify efforts to achieve peace
- Identify historic examples of individual, national, and/or international efforts to achieve peace, and discuss the outcomes of these efforts
- Read the United Nations Charter as the document describes the organization's role in helping the world to achieve peace
- Identify individuals and/or organizations who have contributed to achieving the goal of world peace
- Select a current civil or international conflict where peace is a goal, and suggest steps that could be, or are being, taken to resolve the conflict and avoid further violence
- Draft a model statement for individuals to sign requesting that governments and international agencies work together to secure world peace

Illustrative Examples of Concepts

peace	peace process
conflict resolution	cause/effect
international cooperation	violence/nonviolence
peacemakers/peacekeeping	military intervention
humanitarian assistance	

Illustrative Examples of Skills to Be Developed/Expanded

gathering, analyzing, and interpreting information
describing previous peace efforts and the results of these efforts
identifying individuals and organizations who have promoted and/or strengthened peace and peace efforts
decision making

Procedures for Learning Activity(ies)

1. Ask students to define *peace* and the peace process.

2. Have students identify various peace efforts in the past.

3. Ask students to identify key people, such as Immanuel Kant, Mohandas Gandhi, Woodrow Wilson, and Jimmy Carter, and international organizations, such as the United Nations and its related agencies, that have sought to achieve peace, however limited.

4. Tell students to prepare an oral or written report about these individuals or organizations for sharing in class.

5. Have students examine a current, ongoing conflict and suggest a course of action that could be helpful in achieving peace in the region.

Student Evaluation

Have students select a historic or current conflict and discuss in some detail the causes and effects of the conflict on the local community, state, nation, and international community.

Or

Ask students to examine three or four current conflicts that are creating tensions and decide whether each of these conflicts is local, regional, national, or global. Have students plot these conflicts on a continuum, extending from local to global, and explain why they placed the conflict where they did on the continuum.

Local	Regional	National	Global

War/Conflict Continuum

Or

Let students use a world map to identify and locate where conflicts or wars have taken place over the last five years. Are there regions of the world that are highly involved, marginally involved, or not involved in securing or maintaining their place in the global economic market? Are there conflicts or wars in regions that are seeking political freedom? In some detail, discuss any connections between the location and the reasons for these tensions.

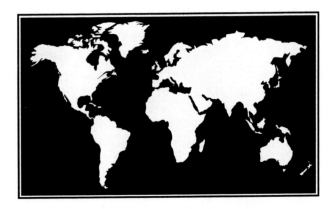

Materials/Data Sources Needed (Teachers/Students)

United Nations Charter

Variety of history and political science reference books

World map (political, physical, regional, etc.)

An Agenda for Peace: The Role of the United Nations. Stanford, CA: SPICE, 1995. (Activity book with reproducible pages and audiocassette)

Basic Facts About the United Nations. United Nations: United Nations Publications, 1995. (The United Nations Charter is included in this publication. This reference is updated on a regular basis.)

Bok, Sissela. *A Strategy for Peace: Human Values and the Threat of War.* New York: Pantheon, 1989

Soldiers for Peace. United Nations: United Nations Publications, 1988. (Paperback and videocassette)

Note: The United Nations Publications are available from the United Nations or from the Social Studies School Service, 10200 Jefferson Boulevard, Room 1421, P.O. Box 802, Culver City, CA 90232-0802.

What Ethical, Social, Political, and Economic Forces Influence the Achievement of World Peace?

For most of our existence, humankind has not known peace. Internal and international conflicts have been ongoing throughout history. Virtually every generation of people has hoped for peace—preferably a lasting peace, which so far has remained elusive. Various individuals and organizations have sought to achieve peace through military action, signing international agreements to guarantee peace, issuing moral statements deploring violence, and offering to mediate disputes. For example, civil conflicts have erupted in recent years throughout the world: in Peru, China, India, Afghanistan, Central America, and elsewhere. International conflicts have occurred in Bosnia, Rwanda, the Persian Gulf, and the Middle East.

1. Define *peace*.

   _____

2. What is the *peace process*? Why is it important?

   _____

3. Identify some people, past and present, who have played key roles in efforts to achieve peace.

   _____

   _____

4. Prepare a report on one of these individuals. Explain the person's contributions to the peace process. To what extent were the peace efforts successful?

   _____

   _____

   _____

   _____

   _____

   _____

   _____

   _____

5. Research a current, ongoing conflict. Suggest a course of action that you believe might help achieve peace in that area.

   _____

   _____

What Ethical, Social, Political, and Economic Forces Influence the Achievement of World Peace?

Choose one of the following. Use the space provided to make notes.

A. Cause and Effect

Select a civil or international conflict—either historic or current. Detail the causes and effects of this conflict on the community, state, nation, and world.

_____

_____

_____

_____

B. Plotting the Conflicts

Identify three or four current conflicts. Decide whether each of these conflicts is local, regional, national, or global and explain your decision. What is a possible outcome of these conflicts?

_____

_____

_____

_____

C. Mapping the Conflicts

Use the world map page to locate places where wars have occurred over the past five years. Describe those places. Then write down your thoughts on any connections between the locations and the tensions.

_____

_____

_____

_____

(continued)

What Ethical, Social, Political, and Economic Forces Influence the Achievement of World Peace? *(continued)*

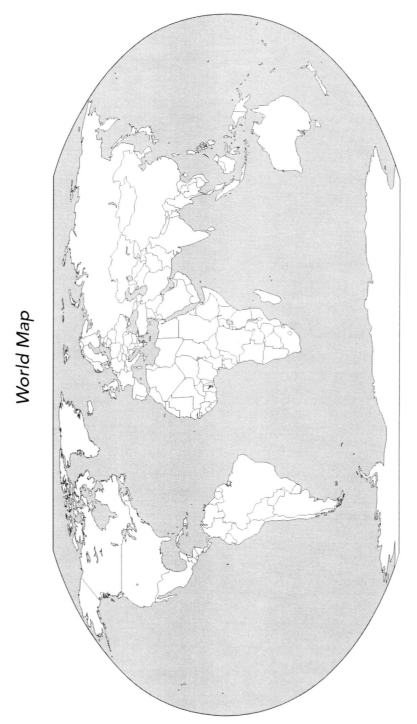

World Map

Organizational Structure of Lesson 10-A

> THEME: Civic Ideals and Practices
>
> TITLE OF LESSON/UNIT (TOPIC):
> Who Should Be Included in a Citizens Hall of Fame?
>
> SUGGESTED GRADE LEVEL/LENGTH OF TIME FOR LESSON/UNIT:
> middle school/two to ten (or more) days

Setting the Context for the Lesson/Unit

Our democracy is based on the thoughts and actions of many people—both women and men—who expressed their ideas and took specific actions, sometimes at great risk, to help envision, build, and maintain our democracy. These women and men (both in the United States and beyond) should be recognized for their contributions to the United States and elsewhere.

Objectives for the Lesson/Unit

Students will

- Identify women and men who have contributed to the creation, development, and expansion of democracy in the United States

- Research from several sources heroines and heroes who have contributed to our democratic nation or democracy in other nations

- As a class, prepare a booklet (including sketches or photographs) about the people identified, and share it with classmates and other students, parents, and interested members of the community

Illustrative Examples of Concepts

> democracy
> heroine/hero
> criteria

Illustrative Examples of Skills to Be Developed/Expanded

> researching
> organizing and interpreting information
> creating and sharing a publication
> making judgments

Procedures for Learning Activity(ies)

Students should discuss the notion of heroine/hero by identifying characteristics of persons who are often referred to as being a heroine or hero. Students should brainstorm a list of persons who are considered to be heroic for various reasons.

You may want to provide an initial list of heroic people (with brief identifying comments) and ask the students to add the names of other persons to the list. The list may well include people in leadership roles, reformers, scientists, educators, authors, medical personnel, inventors, explorers, artists, philanthropists, government officials, and so forth. Ask students to select one person whom they wish to study in some depth and to prepare a report on the person selected. Guidelines as to what (at a minimum) is to be included in the report should be established either by you or by the class as a whole.

For the next several days, allow students research time in the school or local public library. (Be sure the librarians know of this assignment in advance so they will be prepared to help students.) Plan for time to assemble the reports/booklets. The completed reports/booklets should be shared with classmates, other students, families, and community members.

Student Evaluation

The production and sharing of the booklet itself is one type of student evaluation. Of course, a portfolio showing various draft materials could be used as well.
Or
Have students write a brief biography of an imaginary person, indicating why she/he is a heroine/hero and how she/he contributed to the spirit of democracy.
Or
Tell students to write a detailed job description for the office of citizen, which should include qualifications, necessary experiences, job expectations, and so on.

Materials/Data Sources Needed (Teacher/Students)

- List of people who could be considered to be heroines/heroes
- Sufficient reference materials in the school or local public library
- A letter to parents indicating the topics of the unit and tasks involved so that parents can assist their children in the development of the report/booklet
- Supplies to create a publication (art and production supplies needed will depend on the desired level of sophistication)

CIVIC IDEALS AND
PRACTICES
Activity 10-A

Who Should Be Included in a Citizens Hall of Fame?

Our democracy is based on the thoughts and actions of many people—both women and men—who expressed their ideas and took specific actions, sometimes at great risk, to help envision, build, and maintain our democracy. These women and men (both in the United States and beyond) should be recognized for their contributions to the United States and elsewhere.

1. As a class, discuss the notion of a **heroine** or **hero** by identifying characteristics of such individuals.

_____

_____

_____

_____

_____

_____

2. **Name** some heroic people and choose one of them to study in some depth.

3. _____

4. _____

5. _____

6. _____

7. _____

8. _____

9. **Research** your heroic person. Prepare your report. Share it with others.

_____

_____

_____

_____

_____

_____

_____

Name _____ Date _____

Who Should Be Included in a
Citizens Hall of Fame?

Select one of the following projects. Use the space provided to make notes.

A. Booklet

Create a booklet based on your study of a heroic person.

(1) Edit, revise, and illustrate your report on the heroic person.

(2) Add covers and transform the report into a booklet.

(3) Share the booklet with others.

_____

_____

_____

_____

B. Biography

Write a biography of an imaginary person whose life was an example of true heroism.

_____

_____

_____

_____

C. Job Description

Create a detailed job description for the office of citizen.

_____

_____

_____

_____

Organizational Structure of Lesson 10-B

THEME: Civic Ideals and Practices

TITLE OF LESSON/UNIT (TOPIC):
How Do Citizens Influence Campaign Issues and Voters?
What Does It Mean to Be a Citizen of Many Different Institutions at the Same Time?

SUGGESTED GRADE LEVEL/LENGTH OF TIME FOR LESSON/UNIT:
high school/one to five days prior to a local, state, or national election

---

Setting the Context for the Lesson/Unit

Prior to Election Day, candidates for public office indicate to the voters their positions on election-related issues. These positions are reported to the public via the media, rallies, appearances, press conferences, interviews, and so on. In response, voters often express their viewpoints and concerns via letters to the editor, radio talk shows, and at candidate forums. These are examples of democracy in action, citizens participating in the democratic process by helping to shape policy. There are numerous activities (civic work) in which citizens can be involved.

The same principle holds true for controversial issues that may ultimately appear on ballots: decisions about the location of a new airport or prison, increasing the local sales tax to pay for municipal improvements, and so forth. As in other elections, citizens express their opinions with their votes.

Objectives for the Lesson/Unit

Students will

- Study campaign issues/concerns from several perspectives so as to become informed citizens

- Decide their personal positions on issues/concerns being studied

- Express their opinions on selected issues by writing letters to the editor, attending and offering comments in a public issues forum, participating in a radio talk program, distributing campaign/election literature, or engaging in other appropriate political action work

- Examine civic work in political, economic, and social institutions

Illustrative Examples of Concepts

political action
citizenship opportunities/responsibilities
campaign issues
elections
public engagement
civic work
political institutions
economic institutions
social institutions

Illustrative Examples of Skills to Be Developed/Expanded

analyzing information from different perspectives
synthesizing information
evaluating accuracy of information from various sources
articulating opinions/expressions
taking political action

Procedures for Learning Activity(ies)

Several days prior to beginning the unit, ask students to bring in several newspaper clippings from various national, statewide, and local newspapers (news articles, editorials, cartoons, and letters to the editor), or reports and/or commentary from TV and radio reports about the candidates and/or election issues. Candidate or party statements should be included as well. Gather these materials (duplicate clippings are welcome) in a folder for later distribution to students.

As the unit begins, distribute copies of the statements clippings and commentary. Ask students to identify the major candidates and/or issues in the election and to indicate the importance of the issues to the local community, the state, and the nation as a whole. Ask students to identify the individuals and groups/organizations that support or oppose the candidate and/or issue. What reasons are cited for support or nonsupport? How powerful are the arguments used? To what extent are the arguments presented likely to influence voters to support or reject a candidate or issue? Finally, how did the reasons presented influence you? What conclusions could be drawn about the importance of public opinion in shaping public policy issues?

Student Evaluation

Students could engage in a mock political debate, public forum, or radio talk show, discussing the issues/concerns in question.

Or

Student could write a personal letter to the editor of the local press or to a government official describing in some detail their personal opinions on the issues/concerns. In the letter, they should take a stand and urge a particular course of action.

Or

The job of citizen is one of the most important jobs a person is asked to assume. Have students describe three duties of a citizen in the political arena.

1. How can a citizen help articulate a campaign issue?

2. How can a citizen help to influence lawmakers so that the campaign issue becomes a law (or does not become a law)?

3. How can a citizen evaluate the effectiveness of a law, and, if needed, work to change a law?

Responses to these questions could apply to a local or national issue.

Or

Have students create a list of activities and describe the work of a citizen in a social institution; in a political institution at the local, state, or national level; and in an economic institution. What kind of civic work could be expected in each of the three institutions? Citizens have numerous opportunities to serve (work) in social, political, and economic institutions. What are some of these types of activities?

Social Institutions   What are some types of activities citizens may be engaged in while participating in social institutions?

Political Institutions   What are some types of activities citizens may be engaged in while participating in political institutions?

Economic Institutions   What are some types of activities citizens may be engaged in while participating in economic institutions?

What conclusions can be made about citizenship participation?

Materials/Data Sources Needed (Teacher/Students)

Numerous newspaper clippings and candidate's statements about positions on major issues, including news articles, editorials, letters to the editor, pictures, political cartoons, press releases, and so on. If possible, these articles should come from several newspapers and/or media sources and represent varied perspectives on the issues. Both students and teachers should collect these materials.

Information about the election process from various reference materials

Campaign materials from state and local election officials and political parties

CIVIC IDEALS AND
PRACTICES
Activity 10-B

How Do Citizens Influence Campaign Issues and Voters?

Prior to Election Day, candidates for public office indicate to the voters their positions on election-related issues. These positions are reported to the public via the media, rallies, appearances, press conferences, interviews, and so on. In response, voters often express their viewpoints and concerns via letters to the editor, radio talk shows, and at candidate forums. These are examples of democracy in action, citizens participating in the democratic process by helping to shape policy.

The same principle holds true for controversial issues that may ultimately appear on ballots: decisions about the location of a new airport or prison, increasing the local sales tax to pay for municipal improvements, and so forth. As in other elections, citizens express their opinions with their votes.

1. **Collect clippings** on candidates and election issues. Bring them to class.

2. **Identify major races and issues**. List them, and indicate their importance to the community, the state, or the nation.

   _____

   _____

3. **Identify groups and individuals** who support and who oppose the candidates and the issues.

   (a) What reasons are identified for support or nonsupport?

   _____

   _____

   (b) To what extent are the arguments likely to influence you and other voters? How?

   _____

   _____

4. **Draw some conclusions** about how public opinion helps to shape policy.

   _____

   _____

   _____

   _____

   _____

   _____

| CIVIC IDEALS AND PRACTICES
Evaluation 10-B | # How Do Citizens Influence
Campaign Issues and Voters? |

Select one of the following projects. Use the back of this sheet to make notes.

A. Discussion

Stage a mock debate, public forum, or talk show to discuss the issues that are important in the election.

B. Letter

Write a letter to the editor or to a government official. In the letter, express your opinion on an issue or issues, take a stand, and urge a course of action.

C. Job Description

The job of citizen is one of the most important that you are going to assume. Write a paper answering the three questions that follow.

(1) How can you help clarify campaign issues?

_____

_____

_____

(2) How can you influence lawmakers to pass proposed laws that you favor and to defeat proposed laws that you oppose?

_____

_____

_____

(3) How can you determine the effectiveness of laws and work toward changing the laws if need be?

_____

_____

_____

Chapter 5

Additional Resources and References to Enhance Social Studies Teaching and Learning

*For the future to be bright,
It must be lit by the lamp
of learning . . .*

—William A. Henry III

As social studies teachers develop curriculum, decide teaching methods, select instructional materials, create assessment tools to find out what students can accomplish, and organize staff development programs, a wide range of sources are available for thoughtful review and careful consideration. These resources allow teachers to meet the specific needs and interests of young learners in the local school or district. No attempt has been made to identify all of the sources of information that may be helpful to teachers. The resources described and identified in this chapter are a starting point. Teachers are encouraged to go beyond these illustrative examples of references and resources for information to use in the teaching, learning, and assessment of social studies programs.

Professional Organizations

Teachers are encouraged to hold membership in one or more of these social studies-oriented professional organizations. Information about these organizations and their state or local affiliates is available from the national offices.

National Education Association 1201 16th Street NW Washington, DC 20036	American Federation of Teachers 555 New Jersey Avenue NW Washington, DC 20001
Association for Supervision and Curriculum Development 1250 N. Pitts Street Alexandria, VA 22314-1403	Phi Delta Kappa 408 N. Union P.O. Box 789 Bloomington, IN 47402- 0789

The following professional social studies organizations provide a range of information to members—from journals, newsletters, monographs, and bulletins to holding annual meetings, seminars, and workshops (many designed for precollegiate teachers).

The major professional organization for social studies teachers is the **National Council for the Social Studies (NCSS)**. It is composed of more than 22,000 members who include preschool, elementary, middle school/junior high, secondary teachers, administrators, curriculum leaders, social studies supervisors, college and university social science discipline specialists, teacher educators, and others with an interest in social studies and social studies education. The NCSS holds a national conference each November in major cities, and every three years NCSS cosponsors an international conference in various parts of the world, such as Vancouver, Canada; Miami, Florida; Nairobi, Kenya; and Sydney, Australia. The next international conference is scheduled for the Netherlands in the year 2000.

> National Council for the Social Studies
> 3501 Newark Street, NW
> Washington, DC 20016
> http://www.ncss.org

Most states have affiliated state, regional, and/or local social studies councils that promote the interests of social studies educators statewide. For information about these social studies activities and council membership, please contact NCSS, the state social studies specialist at the state education agency, or the social studies methods professor at a nearby college or university. Copies of the NCSS curriculum standards and those published by the other social science discipline organizations are available for purchase from NCSS. The list of standards currently available in civics, geography, history, and economics are included in the reference/resource list at the end of the chapter.

Within the NCSS are four closely affiliated groups. The members of the Council of State Social Studies Supervisors (CS4) are the social studies specialists at the state education agency. The second group are the members of the National Social Studies Supervisors Association (NSSSA) who are district curriculum specialists, instructional supervisors, and others who have similar responsibilities in districts and local schools. The third affiliated group is the College and University Faculty Association (CUFA), which draws its membership from teacher educators, advanced graduate students in social studies, and others involved in teacher education programs. The fourth group is the International Assembly, which is open to NCSS members who desire to collaborate and exchange ideas with colleagues in other nations. Both CUFA and NSSSA have international educators as members, as does NCSS. Included within the NCSS structure are several special interest groups that have sessions during the NCSS annual conference. Some publish newsletters for their members.

The next two organizations offer valuable publications and a range of programs of interest to social studies educators. The Educational Resources Information Center (ERIC) provides the database for social studies and social science education resources, which include articles that have been published in numerous journals and for a range of social studies materials, such as curriculum guides, lesson plans, papers presented at professional meetings, government publications, and so forth. Many of the references are available on computer disks in libraries and other resources centers. ERIC provides a variety of its own publications as well.

The Social Science Education Consortium (SSEC) produces a variety of educational materials on social studies topics for PK–12 educators. The consortium also offers workshops and seminars of interest to social studies teacher educators, social science discipline specialists, curriculum leaders, and others who have contributed to the field of social studies education.

Both of the above social studies organizations have resources that are likely to be of value to teachers and curriculum leaders as they develop and implement social studies standards in the local setting.

ERIC Clearinghouse: Social Studies/Social Science Education Indiana University Social Studies Development Center 2805 E. 10th Street, Suite 120 Bloomington, IN 47408-2698
Social Science Education Consortium (SSEC) P.O. Box 21270 Boulder, CO 80308-4270

Social studies-related adjunct ERIC clearinghouses which have useful topical information for social studies educators include the following. Teachers are urged to contact the individual clearinghouses about publications and services related to these specific topics.

Consumer Education	Law-Related Education	U.S.-Japan Studies
National Institute for Consumer Education 207 Rackham Building West Circle Drive Eastern Michigan University Ypsilanti, MI 48197-2237	Indiana University Social Studies Development Center 2805 E. 10th Street, Suite 120 Bloomington, IN 47408-2698	Indiana University Social Studies Development Center 2805 E. 10th Street, Suite 120 Bloomington, IN 47408-2698

Educators are encouraged to be active participants in the organization(s) related to their area of discipline specialization and/or special interests. In most cases, there are state-affiliated organizations for several of these professional organizations. In many instances, a discipline specialist at the local college or university is likely to be able to provide somewhat detailed information about the organization(s) and other closely related discipline-specific organizations. Some examples of discipline-related organizations follow:

History	
American Historical Association 400 A Street SE Washington, DC 20003	World History Association Department of History and Politics Drexel University Philadelphia, PA 19104
Organization of American Historians 112 N. Bryan Street Bloomington, IN 47408	National Council for History Education 26915 Westwood Road, Suite B2 Westlake, OH 44145-4657

The latter organization promotes the teaching of history in the schools and provides a newsletter to its members.

> National Center for History in the Schools
> University of California, Los Angeles
> 10880 Wilshire Boulevard, Suite 761
> Los Angeles, CA 90014-4108

This center developed and published the national history standards materials.

> National History Day
> University of Maryland
> 0119 Cecil Hall
> College Park, MD 20742

The National History Day organization encourages students in high school to participate in history competitions in one of several categories, such as papers, projects, performances, and media presentations. The competition is judged by professional historians at the district, state, and national levels. The National History Day organization also conducts a three-week summer institute for high school history teachers.

The society serves the needs of historians who fill the role as teacher to various communities of educators. It publishes *The History Teacher* quarterly.

> Society for History Education
> California State University, Long Beach
> Long Beach, CA 90840

Geography	
National Council for Geographic Education Indiana University of Pennsylvania 16A Leonard Hall Indiana, PA 15705	National Geographic Society (NGS) 17th & M Streets NW Washington, DC 20036
Association of American Geographers 1710 16th Street NW Washington, DC 20009–3198	

At present, most states have statewide geographic alliances that provide opportunities for teachers to learn more about geographic content, concepts, and skills, as well as exciting ways to teach young learners about geography and the world. Information about the geographic alliance and alliance coordinators is available from the NGS and/or the state social studies specialist. Many state alliances conduct workshops for teachers, provide staff development programs, and publish newsletters. The NGS develops school curriculum to help improve geographic literacy and the public's understanding of global issues. NGS also sponsors the Geography Bee for students in grades 4–8.

Political Science	
American Political Science Association 1527 New Hampshire Avenue, NW Washington, DC 20036	Constitutional Rights Foundation (CRF) 601 S. Kingsley Drive Los Angeles, CA 90005

The CRF promotes an understanding of citizenship, especially as it relates to the Bill of Rights and it encourages young learners to become active and responsible participants in our democratic society. The foundation provides programs and publications for both young learners and teachers.

Center for Civic Education 5146 Douglas Fir Road Calabasas, CA 91302

The Center for Civic Education developed the civics and government national standards and provides for a variety of other publications related to civic education.

American Bar Association 759 N. Lake Shore Drive Chicago, IL 60611	Close Up Foundation 44 Canal Center Plaza Alexandria, VA 22314

The Close Up Foundation encourages responsible participation in the democratic process, promotes civic awareness, and provides for nonpartisan programs for middle school and high school students. It has available supplemental texts, videos, and teacher guides available.

Economics	
American Economic Association 2014 Broadway, Suite 305 Nashville, TN 37203-2418	National Council on Economic Education (NCEE) 1140 Avenue of the Americas New York, NY 10036

Many states have affiliated state councils for economics education, and within most states there are several centers for economics education. Most state councils and local centers for economics education are located on college and university campuses. Information about the nearest state council or center for economics education is available from the NCEE or a member of the economics faculty at a local university. Both the NCEE and many councils and/or centers offer programs and workshops for teachers and provide a range of instructional materials.

Junior Achievement One Education Way Colorado Springs, CO 80906

Junior Achievement is concerned with developing economic literacy to help ensure our free enterprise system. One of its goals is to impress young people with the value of our free enterprise economic system by offering instructional programs and materials such as Applied Economics and Junior Achievement Company for middle school, junior high, and high school students. Information about these programs, economic education resources, and affiliated state Junior Achievement associations is available from the national office.

Foundation for Teaching Economics 250 Russell Boulevard, Suite B Davis, CA 95616

This foundation promotes economics education by helping economics teachers become more effective. They offer a one-week summer program for selected teachers with leadership potential.

These three behavioral science associations may have some references and resource materials available for precollegiate teachers.

Anthropology	Psychology	Sociology
American Anthropology Association 1703 New Hampshire Avenue, NW Washington, DC 20009	American Psychological Association 750 First Street, NE Washington, DC 20002-4242	American Sociological Association 1722 N Street, NW Washington, DC 20036

In addition to memberships in the professional social studies organizations identified previously, it is recommended that social studies teachers have membership in one or more of the following professional organizations.

National Education Association 1201 16th Street, NW Washington, DC 20036	Association for Supervision and Curriculum Development 1250 N. Pitts Street Alexandria, VA 22314-1403
American Federation of Teachers 555 New Jersey Avenue, NW Washington, DC 20001	Phi Delta Kappa 408 N. Union, P.O. Box 789 Bloomington, IN 47402-0789

Other Sources for Information

State education agencies and local schools and districts often produce excellent curriculum guides and other instructional/reference materials for teachers and curriculum coordinators to review as they implement social studies standards in local schools and classrooms. Some states and districts are in the process of developing assessment tests and establishing proficiency level benchmarks at one or more grade levels. Usually these tests are developed on the basis of national and/or state social studies standards in addition to state and/or district curriculum guidelines.

The Social Studies School Services (SSSS) is a distributor of social studies materials produced by a range of commercial publishers, government agencies, and business organizations. Each year the SSSS produces several catalogs which identify, describe, and illustrate instructional resources that may help educators teach social studies effectively. The SSSS frequently exhibits materials at national, regional, and state social studies conferences.

The publisher of this book, J. Weston Walch, Publisher, has a range of instructional resources that are of help to social studies teachers as they work to implement national and state social studies standards.

For teachers who seek information about specific nations around the world, the embassies, consulates, and national tourist bureaus frequently offer interesting and useful information. Addresses of these government offices and agencies may be found in the yellow pages of telephone directories in large cities such as New York, Washington, DC, San Francisco, Los Angeles, Chicago, and Miami. Local public libraries should also be able to provide such information about various nations.

Most states have an official state tourist bureau (usually located in the state capital), which should be able to provide more detailed information about the state than typical tourist brochures. Some local chambers of commerce also have information about the local community and the nearby region. Given sufficient notice, all of these agencies may be able to provide useful information to both teachers and students.

The Internet is a useful tool for teachers and students in search of information. However, a word of caution is in order: There is little control on the subject matter, the accuracy, and the correctness of what is available on the Internet. Therefore, it may be wise to verify information taken from the Internet with other reliable sources.

It is important to remember that information becomes obsolete very quickly, as does technology. Most professional organizations, agencies, companies, and individuals have Web pages on the Internet.

Teachers should use not only the information provided by the organizations, associations, and businesses identified but also information from other sources they locate on their own, which may offer different perspectives and possibilities. As teachers use this book, they should jot down references with complete citations that will be particularly useful to them as they work on curriculum, instruction, and assessment. The authors would appreciate suggestions of other resource materials that individual social studies teachers find useful.

Standards

Center for Civic Education. *National Standards for Civics and Government.* Calabasas, CA: Center for Civic Education, 1994.

National Center for History in the Schools. *National Standards for History* (Basic Edition). Los Angeles: National Center for History in the Schools, 1996.

National Council for the Social Studies. *Curriculum Standards for Social Studies: Expectations of Excellence.* Washington: National Council for the Social Studies, 1996.

National Council on Economic Education. *Voluntary National Content Standards in Economics.* New York: National Council on Economic Education, 1997.

Geography Education Standards Project. *Geography for Life: National Geography Standards.* Washington: Geography Education Standards Project, 1995.

> **Note:** Copies of these standards may be purchased from NCSS. Ordering information for copies of these standards may be placed by calling toll free at 1 (800) 683-0812 or ordered by fax 24 hours a day at (301) 843-0159.

Additional Readings

Hartoonian, H.M., and M.A. Laughlin. "Designing a Social Studies Scope and Sequence for the 21st Century." *Social Education,* Vol. 53, No. 6, (October). pp. 388-398, 1989.

Joint Committee on Geographic Education. *Guidelines for Geographic Education: Elementary and Secondary Schools.* Washington, DC: Association of American Geographers and National Council for Geographic Education, 1984.

Joint Council on Economic Education. *Master Curriculum Guide: Basic Economic Concepts.* New York: Joint Council on Economic Education, 1984.
(**Note:** The Joint Council on Economic Education is now known as the National Council on Economic Education.)

Laughlin, M.A., and H. M. Hartoonian. *Challenges of Social Studies Instruction in Middle and High Schools: Developing Enlightened Citizens.* Fort Worth, TX: Harcourt Brace College Publishers, 1995.

National Council for the Social Studies. *Standards for the Preparation of Social Studies Teachers.* Washington, DC: National Council for the Social Studies, 1987.

National Council for the Social Studies. "Testing and Evaluation of Social Studies Students." *Social Education.* Vol. 55, No. 5, (September) pp. 284-86, 1991.

Note: Several states and local districts have developed social studies standards and assessment documents, such as curriculum frameworks and planning guides, which should be reviewed.

Notes

Share Your Bright Ideas with Us!

We want to hear from you! Your valuable comments and suggestions will help us meet your current and future classroom needs.

Your name_____Date_____

School name_____Phone_____

School address_____

Grade level taught_____Subject area(s) taught_____Average class size_____

Where did you purchase this publication?_____

Was your salesperson knowledgeable about this product?   Yes_____   No_____

What monies were used to purchase this product?

____School supplemental budget   ____Federal/state funding   ____Personal

Please "grade" this Walch publication according to the following criteria:

Quality of service you received when purchasing ....A   B   C   D   F
Ease of use..A   B   C   D   F
Quality of content..A   B   C   D   F
Page layout ....A   B   C   D   F
Organization of material ....A   B   C   D   F
Suitability for grade level ....A   B   C   D   F
Instructional value...A   B   C   D   F

COMMENTS:_____

_____

What specific supplemental materials would help you meet your current—or future—instructional needs?

_____

Have you used other Walch publications? If so, which ones?_____

May we use your comments in upcoming communications?   ____Yes   ____No

Please **FAX** this completed form to **207-772-3105**, or mail it to:

Product Development, J.Weston Walch, Publisher, P.O. Box 658, Portland, ME 04104-0658

We will send you a **FREE GIFT** as our way of thanking you for your feedback.   **THANK YOU!**